ALECKY BLYTHE

In 2003, Alecky founded Recorded Delivery, whose first production, *Come Out Eli*, premiered at the Arcola Theatre, London. The production won the Time Out Award for Best Performance on the Fringe and later transferred to the BAC as part of the Time Out Critics' Choice Season. The company went on to make *All the Right People Come Here* (New Wimbledon Theatre). Alecky has since created *Strawberry Fields*, a commission by Pentabus; *Cruising* (Bush Theatre, London); *The Girlfriend Experience* (Royal Court Theatre and Young Vic, London); *I Only Came Here for Six Months* for KVS Brussels and the British Council; *Are We Refugees?*, a joint project for the National Theatre Studio and the Rustaveli Theatre, Georgia.

For television she has written *A Man in a Box* for IWC and Channel 4, which was part of their Coming Up Series.

Alecky Blythe

THE GIRLFRIEND EXPERIENCE

NICK HERN BOOKS

London

www.nickhernbooks.co.uk

A Nick Hern Book

The Girlfriend Experience first published in Great Britain as a paperback original in 2008 by Nick Hern Books Limited, 14 Larden Road, London W3 7ST, in association with the Royal Court Theatre, London

Reprinted in this revised edition 2010

The Girlfriend Experience copyright © 2008 Alecky Blythe

Alecky Blythe has asserted her right to be identified as the author of this work

Cover illustration by Syd Brak
Cover designed by Ned Hoste, 2H

Typeset by Nick Hern Books, London
Printed in Great Britain by CPI Antony Rowe, Chippenham, Wiltshire

A CIP catalogue record for this book is available from the British Library

ISBN   978 1 85459 526 3

FSC
Mixed Sources
Product group from well-managed
forests and other controlled sources

Cert no. SGS-COC-002953
www.fsc.org
© 1996 Forest Stewardship Council

The Girlfriend Experience was first performed at the Royal Court Theatre, London, on 18 September 2008, with the following cast:

TESSA	Debbie Chazen
AMBER	Esther Coles
POPPY	Lu Corfield
SUZIE	Beatie Edney
MAN	Alex Lowe

Director	Joe Hill-Gibbins
Designer	Lizzie Clachan
Lighting Designer	Charles Balfour
Sound Designer	David McSeveney

The production transferred to the Young Vic, London, on 29 July 2009 (previews from 24 July).

Introduction

As soon as I met the women at the parlour I knew I wanted to make a play about them. Apart from being immediately likeable, they broke the stereotype of working girls that is presented in the media. Prostitution has had plenty of coverage over the past couple of years for good reason but none of it has addressed this particular niche.

The popular notion of prostitutes is that they are either high-class escorts, drug-addicted street walkers or pimped victims of human trafficking. The women at the parlour, on the other hand, are an entirely different category, but they still represent an important sector in the industry. They are self-employed, middle-aged women carving out a business under their own rules. It is their very ordinariness that makes them and their hidden world so extraordinary to me.

In an increasingly competitive market due to the influx of foreign girls, the women have to sell more than just sex to make a living. The 'Girlfriend Experience' is a service that they offer which is more personal and intimate than the physical act alone. The play explores the ways the 'Girlfriend Experience' impacts upon the women and blurs the boundaries between their work and their private lives.

Special thanks to the women at the parlour who let me into their secret world.

Thanks to Mark Wing-Davey for teaching me the Recorded Delivery writing and performance technique.

A.B.

Characters

THE GIRLS

TESSA, *real age fifty-eight. Striking. Youthful complexion and energy. Gothic ex-dominatrix.*

POPPY, *real age thirty-eight. Scruffy. A carefree, childlike manner. Vulnerable.*

SUZIE, *real age forty-two. Cuddly. Kind, sparkly eyes. Fast talking and a dirty laugh.*

AMBER, *real age thirty-five. Sweet-looking. Cynical and worldy wise.*

THE PUNTERS

VIAGRA MAN, *early sixties. Friendly.*

MARTIN, *mid-forties. Tracksuit bottoms, work boots.*

GOD'S GIFT, *mid-forties. Tennis shorts, blue V-neck jumper.*

MIKE, *late thirties. Smart, dark-grey suit.*

GROPER, *late fifties. Balding, jeans, leather jacket.*

GLOVE MAN, *late seventies. Large girth, high-waisted trousers, walking stick.*

DICKBRAIN, *mid-sixties. Short, beige bomber jacket, slacks.*

TERRY, *early sixties. Tall, slim, grey haired, short-sleeved shirt, Hush Puppies.*

ALECKY, *voice-over. Polite and friendly manner.*

Setting

A basement flat in Bournemouth. The action of the play takes place in the sitting room and the hallway. The view of the hallway is partly obscured. There are two bedrooms off the hallway. The kitchen is off the sitting room. In the sitting room there is a sofa, two armchairs, a television, and a small side table with a phone and a notebook.

Notes

Some names and place names have been changed.

Further physical and costume details for the women can be found in the stage directions, and in the text when they describe themselves to punters over the phone.

The play is to be staged as if the audience were sitting in the room with the women. To this end, much of the dialogue is to be delivered as direct address to the audience.

A forward slash (/) indicates the point at which the next speaker interrupts. When two adjacent lines begin with a forward slash, the dialogue begins simultaneously.

Dialogue starting with a (–) indicates that it follows immediately on from the character's previous line.

Dialogue in [square brackets] is not to be spoken, but is included as a guide to pronunciation.

ACT ONE

Prologue – Technique

ALECKY (*voice-over*). I feel like I should explain – what I'm doing with m-microphones an' stuff like that – / just so that you know –

TESSA. Mmm – We did sort of / – a bit.

POPPY. Yeah –

Beat.

ALECKY (*voice-over*). Um (*Beat.*) – I, um (*Beat.*) – I kindof make (*Beat.*) – um (*Beat.*) – they're sortof documentary plays. (*Pause.*) But – I don't – *film* anything (*Beat.*) – I just re*cord* – hours and hours of-of – audio. (*Pause.*) Um (*Beat.*) – and I – edit it (*Beat.*) – and then, um (*Beat.*) – those (*Beat.*) – so (*Beat.*) – people's *real* words your real words – then become the words that the actors speak in the play – and they, they – *hear* – your voice – speaking – through earphones – and then they *copy* – exactly your intonation, accent – I'll describe – y'know – one was *sat* here, one was sat here, and whatever.

POPPY. Yeah.

ALECKY (*voice-over*). And it's – it's a really weird, kindof very true – obviously *so* so true to *life*, kindof thing –

TESSA. So you 'ave to be careful what you *say* –

They laugh.

SUZIE. So are you gonna have the bed, are you gonna have the living – set as a living room?

TESSA. Yeah?

SUZIE. Then you'll be able to hear off set, you'll be able to hear a door, you'll be able to hear the punter, you'll be able to hear going into a bedroom and the door shutting, so then when they're talking people look at the telly and the audience is out there. (*Beat.*) I'll tell you something that must be nice is that

5

actors – playing real people in real situations. Cuz it must be so – a lot of it is fantasy or fiction – not fantasy it's fiction.

TESSA. Yeah cuz you can make up a character from what your *reading* / and you gotta look and sound and do –

SUZIE. Yeah absolutely and you gotta – you – quite a lots built in – but it must also be quite nice knowing that the person *is* real.

TESSA. Mmmm.

SUZIE. And it's *not* fiction.

TESSA. Yeah. It's getting very real now. Gettin' very scary. This is scary now.

SUZIE. It's exciting.

TESSA. Scary! Please make me tasteful. Ha ha.

SUZIE. A job an' a half that is!

TESSA (*laughs*). I know – that's what I mean.

Scene One – Happy Hookers

Mid-morning, 5th October 2006. SUZIE *enters from the front door.* TESSA *is busy clearing away laundry that is sprawled over the backs of chairs.*

SUZIE. Wow, this looks *good*. / (*Pause.*) This looks *good* – looks *love*ly.

TESSA. Oh God. I'm gettin' there.

SUZIE. You been busy *girly*.

TESSA. Oh I try to be –

SUZIE. I got pressie.

Pause. TESSA *unwraps two pale pink candles in glass candleholders.*

TESSA. Ooh, good. (*Pause.*) Um – ooh, very nice (*Beat.*) – and, um (*Beat.*) – ooh, extra *extra* nice – I like –

SUZIE. One for each room.

TESSA. Thank you.

SUZIE. No it looks nice / (*Beat*.) – that *green* looks really nice.

TESSA. Do you like it? – It dint get done.

    Pause.

SUZIE. Isn't it – gorgeous (*Beat*.) – Isn't it – I mean (*Beat*.) –
Tessa has, um (*Pause*.) – sh, well *she* set all this out cuz it was
all unfurnished when she came (*Beat*.) – and she's done all this,
done all the decorating, got all the furniture in –

    Beat.

TESSA. But the – the *Chesterfield's* s'posed to be coming. (*Pause*.)
'E's *late* with them.

SUZIE. An' I'll, um (*Beat*.) – I'll put these in the room.

TESSA. Okay.

SUZIE. I need to take the plastic bit off is that all right – is that all
right? / D'you like that?

TESSA. That's *love*-ly.

    SUZIE *goes into the small bedroom, followed by* TESSA.

SUZIE. Oh, you've changed *round* in here –

TESSA. Yeah.

SUZIE. Oh fan*tast* – oh that's *better* –

TESSA. Yeah s'a bit bigger, isn't it?

SUZIE. That's better.

TESSA. I thought I could try a / (*Beat*.) – I've got to clean outside.

SUZIE. Put those where you want.

    Pause.

    That is *much* better. (*Pause*.) Oh, it d- makes the room look a lot
bigger –

TESSA. Doesn't – doesn't it.

SUZIE. I need to have to take some more pictures now you've changed the room around.

TESSA. Yeah.

SUZIE. It's c- al*though* nobody actually *lives* here – it's to make it feel *homely* –

TESSA. Yeah – / they like it homely –

SUZIE. An' – an' it's like – you're not – although a guy may only come here – for – like, a twen'y-minute hand job (*Beat.*) – he still gets the same *at*mosphere – and ambience – that everybody else has.

A phone rings.

TESSA (*to audience*). If anybody asks, you're the lady who does the phones, okay?

SUZIE. Jus' say – jus' say you're the maid.

Pause.

Tessa's done so well – I mean, there was nothing here. (*Beat.*) She rents it privately – so the guy just thinks that she lives here. (*Beat.*) So (*Beat.*) – it's – it's (*Beat.*) – I mean people are here every day. (*Beat.*) It's lived in, during the day, just not slept in overnight, normally – so – (*Pause.*) It's just so welcoming (*Beat.*) – it's lovely –

TESSA. I *love* nineteen-thirties, I *love* Art Deco, I'm *very* old-fashioned, I'm I'm sorry I am / I'm not modern –

SUZIE. Nah s'lovely / (*Beat.*) – it's homely –

TESSA. – these are *far* too modern –

SUZIE. Extra bits you've got look really nice –

TESSA. Well, this is it. (*Beat.*) *This* (*Beat.*) – I picked up from the Sally Army / (*Beat.*) – and, I'm –

SUZIE. I like that.

TESSA. – I'm gonna paint it *white* (*Beat.*) – and I've got some paper, *Mel*rose, that matches / (*Beat.*) – I'll – in there –

SUZIE. I'll put – through there. (*Pause.*) – / That'll be nice – it'll be like a dressing room in here.

TESSA. Isn't it? (*Beat.*) – *Isn't* it (*Beat.*) – isn't it? So (*Beat.*) – an' then get a li'le table an' I got another chair –

Pause.

D'ya like that?

She points to a glass lampshade above.

SUZIE. That's lovely I was lookin' at / that earlier.

TESSA. It's – *glass* (*Beat.*) – it's / (*Beat.*) – I thought it was plastic.

SUZIE. 'Ow'd you get it up there? – 'Ow'd you get it *up* there?

TESSA. Uuuuhhhh (*Beat.*) – with great difficulty.

SUZIE. Oh.

TESSA. I've got another one to go in the kitchen. (*Beat.*) – / Guess how much –

SUZIE. You've done loads – you've done / *loads*, here –

TESSA. – *Guess* how much (*Beat.*) – a gl- this is *glass* – embossed gla- / (*Beat.*) – all the bright things stand out.

SUZIE. Where did you buy it from?

TESSA. Wilkinson.

Pause.

SUZIE. Mm I've got no idea six quid.

TESSA. Fifteen.

SUZIE. Fifteen? Oh well – see *usually* – you'd find / (*Beat.*) – you would find that –

TESSA. I – well *I* thought it was plastic –

SUZIE. – you would find that for about – I don't know, for about – forty to between forty and sixty quid / (*Beat.*) – glass –

TESSA. I looked at the g- – the – up the road there's a a a – a 'lectric shop on the corner –

SUZIE. Mm.

TESSA. – uh, eighty-five pound (*Pause.*) – / was the nearest –

SUZIE. Bloody *hell*!

TESSA. – nearest I could see. / (*Beat*.) I thought –

SUZIE. Nice. I like it.

TESSA. Isn't that lovely (*Beat*.) – I couldn't get over that.

SUZIE. S'lovely. What you've done, is lovely.

TESSA. D'you like?

SUZIE. Can't b'lieve you've done so much in two weeks.

TESSA (*sighs*). Oh (*Beat*.) – God. Well I want ma sofas, now. (*Beat*.) I'm putting that sofa, in there (*Beat*.) – I'm moving the table – so we can put the telly-vision on it, and then, you can sort of sit, and chat – and / (*Beat*.) – s'better –

SUZIE. Yeah (*Beat*.) – cuz the longest sessions – aren't just, you know – the guys like to talk to you, as well / (*Beat*.) – there may be a bit of roleplay –

TESSA. Yeah, they 'ave tea – a coffee, yeah –

SUZIE. – they get when they get here they get offered a drink (*Beat*.) – then they can relax an' we leave 'em in the rooms / and they can just –

Beat.

TESSA. Mm-hmm – mm-hmm.

SUZIE. – like – look around the ss – if they're new, / ya know –

TESSA. Yeah. / (*Beat*.) Mm.

SUZIE. – look around the surroundings, jus' relax a bit, before we come an' / – jump on 'em. (*Laughs*.)

TESSA. It's like I have, I have a married couple that come an' see me (*Beat*.) – an' it's lovely, ha (*Beat*.) – w-we have a bottle of wine, and we chat, an' – then do whatever we need to do, and chat again bla- (*Whispering*.) 'See you next week', 'Oh, hi' – an' it's all – (*Double-kiss noise*.) 'Great stuff.'

SUZIE. I ought to get changed, really –

TESSA. Yeah, and me.

SUZIE. You see, I come with a big a little suitcase, every Wednesday, I bring everything with me –

TESSA. Trolley dolly.

SUZIE. Trolley dolly, me.

SUZIE goes to her suitcase and starts unpacking it.

TESSA. She's a trolley dolly –

Pause.

SUZIE. Oh the, oh the *iron* (*Beat.*) – brought the iron –

TESSA. Oh, brilliant –

SUZIE. S'in here.

TESSA. – brilliant.

SUZIE. Trolley / dolly.

TESSA. I was – really naffed off – cuz I've just changed the bedding there – and the oil mark, is still on it – and I'm *really* / annoyed with it (*Beat.*) – so –

SUZIE. Oh, you need – you need to put some – washing-up / liquid on it (*Beat.*) – or some –

TESSA. Yeah I'm gonna get some of that Vanish stuff / (*Beat.*) – an' – and –

SUZIE. – or some Vanish stuff.

TESSA. – an' do it (*Beat.*) – but – it *is* clean.

SUZIE. 'At's okay.

Pause.

I bring – a little towel, I'll bring – my stuff (*Beat.*) – toiletries to freshen myself up with – make-up (*Beat.*) – bring my food supply for the day, me Red Bull (*Beat.*) – condoms – lube, li'le toy, just in case.

Pause.

We come here, get ready in a rush, then nobody knocks on the door for an hour or so. You gotta be – sod's law is, if you're not ready, someone'll knock.

TESSA. Oooh. (*Pause.*) Oh, I've got a story to / tell *you*.

SUZIE. She's gots-store a *story* –

TESSA. Oh-/oh-oh-hooooo.

SUZIE. – a story!

TESSA. This guy, Little Milton Guy we call 'im, he's been – seein'
Amber – what, five y- six years, since she started, right. (*Beat*.)
So, he'd been to the other place, right? Saw this (*Beat*.) – *lap*-
dancer. (*Beat. Pervy laugh*.) He said 'It scared the – crap outta
me (*Beat*.) – uum – no boobs, nothi-' 'e says – 'Oh God, she
was ugly', *any*way –

SUZIE *laughs*.

Uhm. 'E was in there, approximately *eleven* minutes – right
(*Beat*.) – um, he wanted to kiss, that was ten pound extra, 'e
wanted to go down on 'er, that was *twenty* pound extra, he said
'By the time I'd done eleven minutes, I'd spent eighty pound
(*Beat*.) –

SUZIE *gasps*.

– on nothink.' / (*Beat*.) – Right –

SUZIE. Oh my *God*.

TESSA. – I mean, 'e's a sweet little soul – 'e pays sixty pound, 'e's
twenty minutes – ever so easy – anyway – 'e, 'e saw the both of
us, blew 'is brains out – an' said 'Ooh my God that is fantast-
iiiiic (*Beat. Giggles*.) – I'm soo pleased to see *yoooouuu*.'
(*Beat*.) So that's another one that went.

Pause.

SUZIE. See, [th]-is is what the girls are finding, they've *both* come
from the same flat – Tessa came here first to set herself up –
then – Amber has followed her around here. (*Beat*.) The guys
that have seen both Tessa an' Amber – um, obvi'sly they drew –
punters in – and so they're still telling guys that they're still,
working there, but they're not there on the day that they want
them to be / (*Beat*.) – so it's like false advertising –

TESSA. Oh no she ac- (*Beat*.) – she actually told him he was, she
was *there* – on Tuesday, that – that Amber was *there* (*Beat*.) –
right / (*Beat*.) – so 'e phoned –

SUZIE. An' she was 'ere!

TESSA. Yes (*Beat*.) – she was *there* / – right –

SUZIE. She was here!

TESSA. – an' that, um – 'Oh, sorry Amber had to go home – but she's got this, she's got this *lovely* pole-dancer, you must come in and see her.'

SUZIE. But see, gradually, the guys, are now finding out where Tessa – and Amber, are – and they're coming here. (*Beat.*) Cuz that also helps with me doin' the advertising on the internet cuz I've had loadsa people say (*Beat.*) – 'Ooh, is that *so*-and-so, who used to work at so-and-so?' and w-, like – 'Yeah / (*Beat.*) – get yer bum down there because yes it *is*.'

TESSA. Mm-hmm (*Beat.*) – yes.

Pause.

This is a business – where – i-it *is* a business where iss (*Beat.*) – ah-I *want* a give the best I *can* (*Beat.*) – and make people *happy*. (*Beat.*) I was so fed up – wiiith (*Beat.*) – being told what to do and how to do it (*Beat.*) – w-workin' for someone *else* (*Beat.*) – one they're takin' fifty per cent of your *money* (*Beat.*) – fer doing, *fuck* all – basically (*Beat.*) – uuurm (*Beat.*) – and telling yer – ye know, y-y-you've, you've gotta rip 'em off left right and centre – uuurm. (*Beat.*) Girlies – that were doing things, that I didn't ap*prove* of – erm – especially the foreigners – erm, doing everything for nothing. (*Beat.*) So – finding a place on my *own* (*Beat.*) – especially with the back-up of the other two – ladies (*Beat.*) – just made sense.

SUZIE. To get over the first year – is the *hardest* thing – if you can last a *year* –

TESSA. Make or break.

SUZIE. That is the make-or-break time.

Pause.

Go an' 'ave yer shower.

TESSA. Yeah – I'm –

SUZIE. Sort yerself out –

TESSA. Go an' have a shower – get changed (*Beat.*) – become girly.

They laugh.

SUZIE. Transformation time –

TESSA. Yes / it is.

SUZIE. – take yer knickers with ya.

TESSA. I'm takin' me knickers wi' me.

They laugh.

TESSA *exits to the bathroom, knickers in hand.*

The phone rings and SUZIE *answers it.*

SUZIE. He-*llo*? (*Pause.*) Yes we do, we're based near Bournemouth seafront is that convenient for you? (*Beat.*) Yes, okay, we have two different ladies here on different days – the two ladies we have here today, we have Tessa – she's thirty-nine – five foot six, she has long dark hair brown eyes – very busty, thirty-eight double-F curvy dress size – fourteen – very lovely lady, very bubbly, offers most services (*Beat.*) – we also have, Suzie – she's thirty-seven, five foot two auburn hair blue eyes – very busty forty double-D – and curvy dress size eighteen to twenty very, *passionate* – lady – offers the full Girlfriend Experience. Prices start from forty pound, just for normal, hand relief – through to sixty pound for full service for half an hour – the ladies are also genuinely bi-sexual, so if you're after a *duo* service, they are more than happy to do that for you too. (*Beat.*) Um, it's a drop-in service (*Beat.*) – um (*Beat.*) – we, uuuhh ha- – we're here till about eight eight-thirty. (*Beat.*) If there's a gnome on the doorstep it just means the ladies are busy an' jus' to pop back a bit later (*Beat.*) – otherwise, no gnome jus' come an' knock at the door (*Beat.*) – an' you'll be able to see our ladies. (*Pause.*) You're welcome! (*Pause.*) Jus' give us a ring, please do. (*Pause.*) Bye.

She puts down the phone.

He sounded quite (*Beat. Posh voice.*) – well-to-dooo. (*Beat.*) S'a drop-in service they'll jus' come down.

Pause. SUZIE *giggles as she holds up her vibrator, which is inside a furry pouch.*

S'jus' my li'le vibrator. (*Pause.*) I don't bring my big one.

TESSA. *I'm* not using *thaaat*!

SUZIE. It's my Spittles one –

TESSA. It'll get all wet / an' 'orrible!

SUZIE *provocatively pokes the pink vibrator out of the furry pouch.*

SUZIE. No no – it's in *there*!

TESSA. Oh!

They laugh.

SUZIE. Look – it's the *bag* it's in! (*Laughs.*) Stupid woman.

TESSA. I must remind you – there is another radio (*Beat.*) – cassette – / thingy – in the other –

SUZIE. I saw it.

TESSA. – in the room / there.

SUZIE. 'As it got CDs / in there as well?

TESSA. Yeah s'got CDs in there – ready, just to / play –

SUZIE. We got like a li'le CD, radio thingy, in each room – and it's just –

TESSA. Sorry for buttin' in –

SUZIE. – quite nice not jus' – not just for the, ambience – but also – uumm –

TESSA. It cuts the noise / out – from the next door – (*Laughs.*)

SUZIE. Cuts the noise (*Beat.*) – I've warned 'er about you (*Beat.*) – I've *warned* 'er, about you.

TESSA. It's / hil*a*rious.

SUZIE. I've 'ad one guy – couple of weeks ago, tellin' me, *afterwards*, 'e was tellin' me all these sob story – 'bout 'is / – ex-girlfriend –

TESSA. Yep.

SUZIE. – an' / allsorts –

TESSA. Oooh / – it was funny –

SUZIE. – an' she w- – she was list'nin' to it *all*, next door.

TESSA. Yeah.

SUZIE. She goes to me 'You shoulduv ask, / you shoulda charged 'im extra, for the counselling.'

TESSA. I should've done, yeah.

SUZIE. Oh, I'm gonnoo 'ave a sandwich. (*Beat.*) And I bet you, soon as I 'ave a sandwich (*Beat.*) – the door will go.

Beat.

TESSA. Well I'm hoping. (*Beat.*) Yesterday was (*Beat.*) – / we never *stopped* –

SUZIE. How many guys did you have in yesterday –

TESSA. – we never stopped, yesterday, 'ntil about *four*-ish – a*gain*. (*Beat.*) An' then it went (*Beat.*) – quiet. (*Beat.*) Then we did a coupluv extras, and that was *it*. (*Beat.*) We 'ad about (*Beat.*) – ten, twelve? – through the door?

Pause.

So (*Beat.*) – it *should* (*Beat.*) – *should* pick up.

Pause.

I've always looked at this as not (*Beat.*) – *anything* but a career. (*Beat.*) This *is* my career – this is my job, it's like going down to Sainsbury's and putting things on the shelf, it's *exactly* – the same thing I just do a different thing. But to me this is a *job* – I clock in, I clock out, it's as simple as that. (*Pause.*) It's – like I say, it is my career, it's something that I – actually enjoy doing, / to a point.

SUZIE. And it's / your choice.

TESSA. – *Yes* – it is – it has to be, my choice, if I didn't want to do it, I wouldn't do it –

SUZIE. I mean there *are* easier ways to make / money –

TESSA. Oh –

SUZIE. – but not as much money but there / *are* easier ways.

TESSA. There *are* easier ways, yeah – I'll go out an' get a job any time I like (*Beat.*) – but it'ss – it suits me, at the moment, at the moment, I'm quite happy.

SUZIE. You know, you do it a few times, and you think – 'Well actually – I can do this / (*Beat.*) – I can *do* that – '

TESSA. I can do this – yeah. / (*Beat.*) Yeah, it *is* – it's –

SUZIE. You know, it gives you confidence.

TESSA. You become – an-other person. (*Beat.*) It's, like –

SUZIE. *You*, fundamentally, / but with a different layer –

TESSA. Yeah, a (*Beat.*) – yeah, *yeah* – it's a stage – (*Softly.*) It is a stage. (*Beat.*) And you go an' (*Whispers.*) – *create*.

The doorbell rings.

Beat.

Here we go.

TESSA *exits the sitting room and goes to answer the door.*

SUZIE. Oh God, I'm not ready – shut the door.

TESSA *is in the hallway, just about to open the front door.*

TESSA (*calling*). Can you shut the door?

SUZIE *shuts the door from the hallway to the sitting room.* TESSA *giggles as she opens the door to one of her regular punters,* VIAGRA MAN.

Do as you're told.

TESSA *shows him into a bedroom and enters the sitting room.*

(*Whispering.*) Oh God – it's Viagra Man. (*Pause.*) Oh – 'e takes for *ever*. (*Pause. Still whispering.*) 'E *is* a pain. (*Beat. Laughing.*) I shall be sweatin' buckets when I come out, don't worry.

Pause. SUZIE *puts on some deodorant spray. She coughs slightly.* TESSA *goes into the kitchen and re-enters the sitting room with a pair of tights and some scissors.*

(*Still whispering.*) I need this cuz 'e 'as to tie his balls up, okay? (*Beat.*) Put an Arab-strap on (*Beat. She starts to talk slightly louder.*) – uumm (*Beat.*) – else I'll never get 'im to cum. (*Beat.*) He's just a pain in the neck (*Beat.*) – he really is.

She exits the sitting room.

Oh – dear.

As she enters the bedroom we can hear soothing, ambient music.

Mm, ready –

The door shuts.

SUZIE. I think cuz I'm so focused on making sure my dad's okay (*Beat.*) – and because I know – he's (*Beat.*) – probably not gonna be a*round* (*Beat.*) – five years, max (*Beat.*) – and it may not even be that (*Beat.*) – so all I'm thinkin' about is – doing this, lookin' after my dad – making sure I've got an income. (*Beat.*) Then, when he's gone – um – all I, I don't – all I can think about *then*, is that – I've got other things in place – that, will (*Beat.*) – see me through that. (*Beat.*) Like the counselling – and maybe a little bit of escorting, and then – just see where my options lie and what I want to do. You never know, summink may – happen – I may win the lottery, 'oo knows? (*Beat.*) Who knows wha- I can't think at that far ahead (*Beat.*) – because I'm just so focused on – making sure – I'm earning a living and looking after my dad. (*Beat.*) Mm.

Yeah and I do just kinda live, live for now at the moment, y'know the bills are being paid, my dad's okay, I'm doing what I need to do, you know and I'm having a good life an' it's, you know I wouldn't have missed this phase of my life for anything. I have a bloody good laugh with some of my clients most of my clients know where the boundaries are, we have a good giggle and a good laugh and I'm treated better than some boyfriends have treated me in the past.

You can have good friendships, I mean I've got some really lovely friendships with clients, but that's it. Okay the guy wants to take me for lunch then have an hours paid time with me, I allow that I would never just go out for lunch or dinner with a guy. I won't ever consider it. You have to have boundaries. Either you see me as a client, or you don't see me at all.

I mean I had, um-uuuhh – this four-hour guy, Derek, who bought me the flowers and chocolates and wine and everything – he was like, you know – I – I – 'Well why won't you da-[te]', you know, he was asking me out for a date, and I said, 'I won't,

I *will not* – step across that line' – I said 'because then it gets very *blurred* – because A) you were then – you were a client – then you want to date, so then you're dating, and you get free sex,' I said 'be honest with you, I w- – I, I get, good sex – bad sex, mediocre sex – I get all the sex I need – so for me to be *interested* in someone, has to be more than sex.' (*Beat.*) You see? (*Beat.*) And I said to him, 'I will never *ever* date a client.' (*Beat.*) Never do it. (*Pause. She's listening out for* TESSA.) It's gone fairly quiet – actually, I can't hear 'er. (*Beat.*) Usually I sit 'ere, I can 'ear her. An' it's bec-[ause] –

Pause. The doorbell goes.

Oh, shit.

Suddenly, SUZIE *has to spring into action. She puts down her sandwich and gets into her fluffy mules.*

(*Whispering.*) Okay?

SUZIE *goes to answer the door.*

Suddenly, we can, indeed, hear TESSA.

TESSA (*off, throes of passion*). Oh, yy-*yeah* – yeah.

SUZIE *opens the front door to a punter.*

SUZIE. Hi, step in. (*Beat.*) You 'kay there?

MARTIN. Yeah not too bad, thanks.

SUZIE. Hi, I'm Suzie, have you come to see someone in particular?

The door shuts.

MARTIN. Uuh, both of you, if you're ready? (*Beat.*) / Hm?

SUZIE. Right, um, Tessa's actually *with* somebody, and she's gonna be ready in about quarter of an hour, / but if you want to see both of us, you want to come back in quarter of an hour –

TESSA (*in background, throes of passion*). O-*oh*! (*Beat.*) *Y-yeah* –

MARTIN. I-I'll see you / (*Beat.*) – yeah, that's –

SUZIE. Yeah – okay, come with me.

They head to the other bedroom.

TESSA (*in background*). O-*oh*!

SUZIE. Okay. (*She giggles, suggestively.*) Make yourself com*fy*. /
(*Beat.*) Okay, what can kind of service are you after sweet'art?

TESSA (*in background*). O-oh –

MARTIN. Uh, bit of everything?

SUZIE. Bit of everything, what, for half an hour?

MARTIN. Yep.

TESSA (*in background*). / Ohh –

SUZIE. / Sixty. (*Beat.*) And your name is?

MARTIN. Martin.

TESSA (*in background*). O-*oh* – / y-*yeah* –

SUZIE. I'll just go and freshen up. Can I get you a drink or anything?

MARTIN. No I'm fine thank you very much –

TESSA (*in background*). *Oh* –

SUZIE. Make yourself comfy.

> SUZIE *leaves him in the bedroom and enters the sitting room.*
> *She hides away the money he has just paid her in her suitcase*
> *and picks up her toiletry bag.*
>
> (*Whispering.*) Okay. (*Pause.*) We need to switch this on (*Beat.*)
> – it now goes to answerphone. Okay?
>
> *She exits to the bedroom.*
>
> *Pause.*
>
> *We can hear Westlife playing on the television in the background.*
> *The phone starts to ring. A beep as the answerphone picks up.*

TESSA (*voice on the answerphone*). Hello, we *are* here, we're just
a little bit busy and can't get to the *phone* right now (*Beat.*) –
please try again. Thank you very much – ba-*bye*!

> *Another beep.*

TESSA (*off*). Yeah – o-*oh-oh-oh* – I'm – coming – coming coming
(*Growls.*) coming (*Beat.*) – (*Grunts.*)

> VIAGRA MAN, *off, grunts.*
>
> (*Off.*) O-*ah* – *ah* –

VIAGRA MAN (*off*). Ah –

SUZIE *and* MARTIN *come out of the bedroom and walk to the front door.*

SUZIE. Okay my sweet, I'll show you out. (*Pause.*) You take care have a good weekend, mwah, bye.

MARTIN. Bye.

Pause.

SUZIE *returns to the sitting room.*

TESSA (*off*). Yeah – ooh oh –

Pause.

SUZIE *drops her 'nappy sack' into the bin, as the women do after every client.*

SUZIE (*sighs, a sound not dissimilar to some of those above*). O-*ah* (*Beat.*) – I'm all of a dither now, he was a quick one, he was like – bitathis-bitathat, duh-duh-duh, 'Right, better put the condom on, now' – 'Oh, all right then.' (*Laughs. Pause.*) Yeah (*Beat.*) – paid for half an hour – dunt get a refund.

Pause. She's listening to TESSA *in the other room.*

(*Whispering.*) There's her – she's tryin' to make him to cum in the other room – and I'm, cuz he's seen Tessa before – I said, 'I'm sorry 'bout –' I said, I says, 'This is like *porn*, without the visuals.' 'E was laughing (*Beat.*) – and, uh – she's still it and she's – she's saying to the guy (*Beat.*) – 'Now, *now*, I want you to cum *now*' because obviously he isn't – cuz he's taken Viagra, 'e's probably 'ad a *wank* before 'e came –

Beat.

TESSA *and* VIAGRA MAN *exit the bedroom and go into the hallway.*

VIAGRA MAN (*off*). Thank you very much. Good to see ya. Look after yourself.

TESSA. I certainly will, don't get browner. Bye.

TESSA *enters the sitting room.*

(*Breathing heavily.*) Oh, God that Mr Viagra.

SUZIE. Is 'e did 'e pay for an hour?

Beat.

TESSA. No –

SUZIE. Well 'e fuckin' well shoulda done (*Beat.*) –

TESSA (*really gasping for breath now*). Don't worry I'll take it out on 'im next time.

TESSA *is fixing her hair when the doorbell goes. She exits the room and goes to answer it.*

GOD'S GIFT. Hi (*Beat.*) – it's *you*!

TESSA. It's *me*!

GOD'S GIFT. Bloody *hell*.

TESSA *laughs loudly, coquettish.*

TESSA. How's you?

GOD'S GIFT. Well I see you'd left from there so I was two tim-[ing] as I wanted to go back there.

TESSA. No, not, don't live – don't. Don't live there any – Don't work there any more.

GOD'S GIFT. My God. / (*Beat.*) Well that's a really good surpr-[ise] – pleasant surprise.

TESSA. How's *you*?

GOD'S GIFT *laughs.*

– yeah – well, come on then, get in / here –

GOD'S GIFT. It's good to *see* you –

TESSA. *Yeah*, it's good to see / you –

GOD'S GIFT. So you on your own?

TESSA. No, no, I have another lady with me, do you wanna say 'ello?

GOD'S GIFT. Can do.

TESSA. Yeah. / I'll send her in.

SUZIE *is just about to tuck into her sandwich.*

SUZIE. Oh fucking hell!

GOD'S GIFT. Can't be as good as you though.

TESSA. Ooh, I dunno. I dunno.

GOD'S GIFT *stands in the hallway as* TESSA *pokes her head into the sitting room.*

Come on Suzie, say 'ello.

SUZIE. Let me get me feet on.

Pause.

TESSA. Ya *feet*?

SUZIE *shuffles around to find her fluffy mules.*

SUZIE (*whispering*). What's 'is name?

TESSA (*under her breath*). I don't know.

Pause.

(*Louder now.*) Very nice man – *very* nice man.

GOD'S GIFT *chuckles.*

Dirty bastard, but very nice man –

GOD'S GIFT (*as he comes in*). I beg you pardon, how are you?

SUZIE. Hello.

TESSA *laughs.*

GOD'S GIFT. Hello it's nice to *meet* you.

SUZIE (*kissy noise*). M-wah. M-wah. I'm Suzie – you all right – m-wah – ooh, *two* kisses!

GOD'S GIFT. Of *course.*

SUZIE. You okay?

GOD'S GIFT. Yes I'm fine, thank you / (*Beat.*) – um –

SUZIE. So you seem quite pleased to see our Tessa –

GOD'S GIFT. *Yeah* / – well it's funny – cuz –

SUZIE. Now you've discovered where she is –

GOD'S GIFT. *Yeah*, because it was – and, by chance –

SUZIE. Mm.

GOD'S GIFT. – cuz she left the other place, and I thought, 'A-ahr' –

SUZIE. Didn't know where she was.

GOD'S GIFT. I actually booked to go there, and I phoned here (*Beat*.) – just – her voi-[ce] – yes it was the *voice* that did it, ya know.

SUZIE. Your voice / that did it –

TESSA (*putting on a deep voice*). It was my voi-[ce] (*Beat*.) – it was my voice.

They all share a laugh.

My / voooice –

SUZIE. She's a bit unique, isn't she?

GOD'S GIFT. Yeah.

TESSA. Oh I'm gonna 'ave to change my voice, 'Ello dar-*lin'* / – 'ello –

SUZIE. Nah, put yer French accent on –

TESSA (*French accent*). 'Ello dar-*ling* –

SUZIE. 'Ere ya go, see.

TESSA (*French accent*). *Bonjour madame.*

SUZIE. Yeah, and –

TESSA *and* SUZIE *giggle.*

GOD'S GIFT. So, yeah, so that's it, so it's just – really luck (*Beat*.) / – Well expensive, but – what the hell.

Beat.

TESSA. So what (*Beat*.) – what – what d'ya want?

GOD'S GIFT (*sighs*). Ah-everything, no / – just want a massage –

TESSA *giggles.*

TESSA. Yeah – yeah / (*Beat*.) – yeah, yeah, yeah –

GOD'S GIFT. – that's all I can afford at the moment anyway, to be honest with you, so, uh –

TESSA. – yeah – forty quid, yeah, / no problem –

GOD'S GIFT. Okay – fine.

TESSA. Which lady?

GOD'S GIFT. Well, I don't know, I –

SUZIE. Have Tessa – have Tessa –

GOD'S GIFT. Yeah but I think you're nice / too –

TESSA. She is, she's / gorgeous –

SUZIE. I'm here on a Wednesday – come down on a Wednesday and see / me –

GOD'S GIFT. I can't, I'm going back out to America for a – a month – at the end of the week, so –

TESSA (*sarcastically*). Travels to America…

GOD'S GIFT. I'm really bad – ahh –

SUZIE. Mmm (*Beat.*) – toss a coin.

Pause.

TESSA (*softly*). Go on. (*Beat. Very suggestively.*) Toss.

The girls share a laugh.

SUZIE. Yeah, pay some money an' have a / toss.

TESSA *and* SUZIE *continue to laugh.*

GOD'S GIFT. Shame I haven't got enough money for *both*.

SUZIE. We do *do* duo service, when you back / (*Beat.*) – from the States?

GOD'S GIFT. I haven't got a coin (*Beat.*) – sorry?

TESSA. Haven't / got a coin.

GOD'S GIFT. I don't know yet, but it'll probably be, I don't know, month or so –

SUZIE. Well / we're here/ – so –

GOD'S GIFT. Thank you. You've got a lovely fa-[ce] – well, you've both got lovely faces, but you've got a very / nice face.

SUZIE. Thank you –

GOD'S GIFT. S'all right. (*Beat*.) Uum –

TESSA (*softly*). She's good.

GOD'S GIFT. Good as you?

TESSA. Uh-yeah. She's gorgeous.

GOD'S GIFT. It's the techniques – the thing.

TESSA. She's gorgeous. Okay then.

TESSA. Yeah?

SUZIE. Yeah?

GOD'S GIFT. Yeah (*Beat*.) – / we'll give it a whirl –

SUZIE. Okay – I'll just go and grab my stuff. I won't be a minute.

GOD'S GIFT. Okay.

   Beat.

   TESSA *giggles*.

SUZIE. Sorry what was your name, darl'?

GOD'S GIFT. Simon.

SUZIE (*softly*). Okay Simon.

   GOD'S GIFT *goes into the big bedroom*. SUZIE *enters the sitting room to pick up her toiletry bag*. TESSA *goes to use the bathroom to freshen up*.

   (*Whispering cheekily*.) She's so naughty. (*Hums gently*.) Massage and hand relief. See you a bit later.

   TESSA *passes her in the hallway*.

TESSA. Go get 'em girl. (*A growl*.) Grra!

SUZIE (*entering the bedroom*). Do you want a drink or anything?

GOD'S GIFT. No I'm fine thank you.

SUZIE. You all right?

GOD'S GIFT. Yes. It's very kind. (*Beat.*) Do I get the same?

SUZIE. I don't know what you *get* from 'er (*Beat.*) – you're going to have to get what you get from me!

GOD'S GIFT. I think I'll have her.

SUZIE (*still giggling*). You can't change yer mind (*Beat.*) – 'alfway through –

The bedroom door shuts.

TESSA (*whispering in the sitting room*). He's a bit of a piss-taker. (*Beat.*) Yeah, mm, hee – thinks he's, God's gift to women. He's all mouth and no trousers. (*Beat.*) Yeah, he just likes (*A growl.*) – rr-*aarr*! (*Laughs.*) So hopefully she'll give him 'rr-ahr'! (*Laughs.*) No, she'll handle 'im – no problem at all. (*Beat.*) That's cool (*Laughs.*) He *really* thinks he's it – and 'e's *not* (*Beat.*) – believe me, he is *not*. (*Beat.*) It's like –

The phone rings and TESSA *answers it.*

Hello, can I help you? (*Pause.*) Y-*yeah*, certainly – uh, we've got the lovely Suzie – very voluptuous and very busty, she's a forty double-D (*Beat.*) – uum, we also have Tessa – uh, very busty as *well*, she's a forty double-F. (*Beat.*) O-kay, uum so I'm afraid it's Death by Boobs. (*Pause.*) Okay – ba-bye!

She puts down the phone.

Guy come last week, 'e'd like to come again this week yeah. (*Pause.*) 'I'm in Dorchester at the moment.'

Pause. SUZIE *enters, wearing just a towel and holding her clothes.*

SUZIE. He wants you.

TESSA. Oh.

SUZIE. I'm not doing it for 'im.

TESSA. What?

SUZIE. I'm not turning him on.

TESSA (*whispering, half-laughing*). Oh yerr joking?

Pause.

SUZIE (*whispering*). No. (*Beat.*) Bastard.

TESSA *goes into the bedroom.*

TESSA. Mm – what's the matter with my lady?

GOD'S GIFT (*off*). Nothing – she's just not very –

The door shuts.

SUZIE *sighs. Pause.*

SUZIE (*softly*). I'm not turning 'im on. (*Pause.*) So I said to 'im –
'Now d'you want to start m-massage' 'Yeah, yeah okay – '
'Hands, oil or whatever' 'E said 'No no, prefer – very gently
touch with the hands.' (*Beat.*) So – take all my clothes off 'part
from my knickers and my, thingies, he's naked on the bed – so
I'm giving 'im a really nice, gentle – touching massage –
between the legs, everything, and just gently, how 'e asked me
for it (*Beat.*) – and I could see it, could *feel* that – he just wasn't
responding. (*Beat.*) And 'e says, 'I (*Sighs.*) – I got to tell you,' he
said, 'you're just not doing it for me – ' 'E said 'S'not you –
don't wasn't it's not you (*Beat.*) – I rather, I'd rather see Tessa.'
So I jus' – just jumped off the bed, gathered up my clothes and
came in 'ere. (*Pause. Then, laughing.*) I've sent 'er in there to
sort 'im out. (*She chuckles for a few beats. Sighing.*) Yeah.
(*Pause.*) He said 'It's just cuz I know, I've seen Tessa before and
I know what' I said 'Well you should've asked for Tessa from,
from the be*gin*ning then.' (*Beat.*) I said, 'Each girl's different'
(*Beat.*) – I said, 'my touch is different, to somebody else's
touch.' (*Long pause.*) I don't mind, I don't take that *personally* –
cuz I know, it's not, it's not *me*. (*Beat.*) I know it's *him*. (*Long
pause.*) First time that's ever 'appened to me. (*Beat.*) I said 'Why
didn't you choose Tessa?' (*Beat.*) I said 'We gave you the *choice*.
(*Beat.*) I said it's no skin off my nose if you want to choose
Tessa.' (*Long pause.*) But – 'e can only afford forty quid (*Beat.*)
– massage and hand relief – so he's – he gives it the big all-I-am
– but 'e obviously doesn't, does 'e? (*Beat.*) He obviously isn't, is
'e? (*Beat.*) He's just a, just shows you what a bastard he is.

Scene Two – Love Hurts

Lunchtim. 7th February 2007. TESSA *is changed for work. She has on her glasses and is reading the instructions for a flat-oack CD rack which is currently splayed across the floor.*

She picks up a screw and the instructions.

TESSA. Well where does that bit go then? Oh dear. (*Beat.*) Me and my daughter yeah will be moving here on the last weekend of their school holidays. Everything's planned to move here so we'll be *living* here. (*Pause.*) I'm giving up the house that I – renting at the moment (*Beat.*) – well it, ah, I have to pay, for two lots – An' it's, like – (*Strangling noises.*) killing me – So, this'll be – really *cool*. She's at school still, obviously, she's got another two years – u-uht – to go – And cuz we'll be finishing at seven, she's going round to 'er sister's, which is round the corner – so by the time she finishes school, four o'clock (*Beat.*) – she can go to 'er sister's, or, her boyfriend's, and then – I can pick 'er up. Obvi'sly we never talked, in front of 'er – about it, she just – obvi'sly, *knows* (*Beat.*) – what goes on. (*Beat.*) She's, she's *six*teen she's not stupid. (*Beat.*) Oh, she can't wait, she's going (*High-pitched voice.*) 'A-ah! Big bedroom! (*Beat.*) Yay!'(*Laughs.*) It shouldn't be a problem, the bedding will be changed – separate – so everything will get separate (*Beat.*) –

TESSA *giggles.*

Looking back at the flat-pack.

Right next bit. Oh God…

She starts to assemble the flat-pack.

The phone rings.

Push off. Oh. Bollocks I'm going.

Goes to pick up the phone.

Hello can I help you? Hello? (*Beat.*) Ooh are we working today? Obviously we are.

She puts the phone down and dials 1471.

Please don't. Not today. Yep. (*Writing down the number*.) Oh no I can't deal with him today. I really can't. 'Sall right, phantom caller. I'm gonna 'ave the phone – tapped. (*Beat*.) This 'as been going, for (*Beat*.) – months – here. (*Beat*.) He'll ring once, put the phone down – ring it twi-[ce] (*Beat*.) – put the phone.

Beat.

She stands over the phone waiting for him to ring again. He doesn't so beaten she goes back to the flat-pack.

Oh I've lost me allen key. Oh there it is. Right.

The phone rings.

He-llo can I help you? Oh don't you dare. (*She hangs up*.) Don't you *dare*! Oohh. He's just driving us mental he does this every single day now. But it's just so annoying cuz he keeps doin it now and there's nothing I can do until I can catch the little bastard. I don't want to retaliate. I don't want – I don't *need* the hassle.

He's pushin'.

POPPY *enters from one of the bedrooms*.

Cool? / Uh.

POPPY (*laughs*). He enjoyed that. (*Laughs*.) He did cum in my mouth, though.

TESSA. Oh, did 'e?

POPPY. Slightly – yeah. (*Beat*.) I got fuckin' spunk in me knickers (*Beat*.) – as well –

TESSA *laughs*.

Good job I've got a spare pair innit?

TESSA. Well she hasn't worked very long, she's only been in the business for about five or six *months* – Cuz she's very new. She's just finding things out. (*Beat*.) She's never worked in a parlour before.

POPPY. No this is my first experience. (*Beat*.) Do you drink? (*Pause*.) I've got some – cream sherry (*Beat*.) – I've got a cup of tea as well, but I'm sure it's cold by now.

Pause.

TESSA *picks up another piece of the flat-pack.*

TESSA. I don't know what this is?

Pause. POPPY *stares at the television.*

I've got a *couple*, comin' on Friday –

TESSA. Oh, yeah?

POPPY. – for a booking. (*Beat.*) For two hours –

TESSA *laughs.*

– and, he wants me ta squash her, and, that's what they keep goin' on about.

TESSA. Oh my / (*Beat.*) – *God!*

POPPY. They want me a put on weight. (*Beat.*) – an' – watersports, yeah so that'll be fun, I like that. (*Beat.*) I'm not off'rin' hard sports any more, though (*Beat.*) – it's too much bloody hassle. (*Beat.*) Hard sports is (*Beat.*) – pooin' – basically. (*Beat.*) Cuz I had a – enquiry, last week, about that. (*Beat.*) And he said, 'Ah – I like the really, runny kind, so would you –

TESSA. / Urgh!

POPPY. / – would you be prepared to take (*Laughing.*) laxatives?'

TESSA. Oh-*urgh*! (*Beat.*) / God!

POPPY. An' then 'e said – and I said 'Well, where are you?' – 'e said, 'I'm in *Card*iff.' / (*She laughs.*)

TESSA. *Cardiff!* (*Beat.*) 'You fuckin' stay in *Cardiff* / pal!'

POPPY. Yeah.

The phone rings and TESSA *answers it.*

TESSA. Hello, can I help *you*?

The caller hangs up.

Oh it's getting borin' now. Borin' borin' borin' borin'. More Wednesday 13th? Did you like the music the other day? Shall we put it on? I tell you what. You phone me back and I'll put it on for ya. Okay? I'll set it up for 'im.

She goes to the kitchen to get the CD player.

It is that client.

POPPY. D'you reckon you know whi-, wh-who it is, then?

TESSA. Oh, yeah. (*Beat.*) He's a van driver. 'E's infatuated. (*Beat.*) 'E's – absolutely, infatuated (*Beat.*) – he's a fuckin' screw loose – which means 'e's dangerous.

Pause. With the CD player set up, TESSA *stands over the phone willing it to ring.*

Come on Billy. Ring, *ring*!

Pause.

The flat-pack is not taking shape.

POPPY. I'll bring me wigs next week – shall I bring me wigs, next / week.

TESSA. Oh – yeah, let's 'ave a wig day! Yeah bring 'em on Valentine's Day, yeah, yeah.

Pause.

POPPY. It's gone a bit quiet now, ha'n't it?

TESSA. It *has*. They're all waitin' fer Suzie (*Beat.*) – oh, so she's all *loved up*! (*Sing-song, mimicking* SUZIE.) 'Derek! (*Beat.*) A-ah! Derek!' She sat in here the other day and it was like – f- text after fuckin' *text*, 'Oh I *love* you my d- oh!' / (*She makes vomit sounds.*) – 'Stop doing this, Suzie, for God's sake', she was hysterical.

Pause.

Cuz it is a golden rule – that you do *not* (*Beat.*) – go *out* with, punters. (*Beat.*) It is – because it *never* – *works*. (*Beat.*) An' at the end of the day (*Beat.*) – he is a client, he is a punter, and he will always *be* – a *punter*.

POPPY. Cuz she 'as fallen for him – / definitely.

TESSA. Oh, she has – now – she is – in – deep, now. (*Beat.*) She's even stopping (*Beat.*) – nn-nn – turning away work, so she can be with him, so 'e can *be* there – it's *always* the girl, who gets the crunch.

Pause.

Oh phone back you bastard.

SUZIE *arrives with her suitcase. She has a cold.*

SUZIE. Hello.

TESSA. She's here –

SUZIE. She's here.

TESSA. She's here –

SUZIE. Y'all right –

TESSA. Yeah.

SUZIE. Hello / hello.

POPPY. Sorry I've nicked your seat.

SUZIE. Nah-nah-no – don't worry –

They all share a laugh.

I don't have a seat –

Beat.

TESSA. I don't know how she does it.

Pause.

SUZIE, *hankerchief in hand, coughs and plonks herself down on the sofa.*

SUZIE. I went back to bed this afternoon cuz I went to the doctors' this morning, and I didn't see my normal doctor, cuz they were booked up.

TESSA. Oh you eventually went good.

SUZIE. So I got penicillin, it's difficult when you can't breath and you're giving a blow job. (*Laughs.*) 'Ad this *gorgeous* guy yesterday (*Beat.*) – erm I cancelled him when I had the cold the first time, I thought 'I can't cancel him again' so he came over yesterday (*Beat.*) – oh, God – an' it was like a (*Beat.*) – Adonis –

TESSA. A-*oh*!

SUZIE. Oh my / *word*!

TESSA. You coulda brought 'im 'ere.

SUZIE. He was *gorgeous* (*Beat.*) – dimples –

TESSA *gasps*.

– in 'is chin / 'n' 'is cheeks –

TESSA (*gasps*). A-*oh*!

SUZIE. – blue eyes, an' 'e just was like – 'Oh my God, oh my God – you sure you wanna see me?'

TESSA *laughs*.

Oh – / dear.

POPPY. Ah-introduce 'im? (*Beat.*) Introduce / 'im –

SUZIE. No – you're not 'avin' 'im. / 'E's from Essex –

TESSA. Come on. / Oh no, you're loved up –

SUZIE. He's up from Stansted (*Beat.*) – no –

POPPY. Y-you can introduce 'im.

SUZIE. *No* (*Beat.*) – I can still 'ave good sex, it's allowed.

TESSA. Oh, bollocks.

SUZIE *giggles*.

Tha's not *fair*.

SUZIE. 'E likes me to 'ave good sex (*Beat.*) – an' then tell 'im about it. (*She giggles.*)

TESSA *tuts*.

I've 'ad this *client*, Derek, he's single – he's age forty-eight (*Beat.*) – I've 'ad 'im since the end of (*Beat.*) – well – about – June-ish, I suppose (*Beat.*) – come – once a month, for *four* hours. (*Beat.*) Always brings flowers, always brought chocolates (*Beat.*) – an' then – New Year's Eve, he – text me – and said, uh – 'Just wish you Happy New Year, before everything gets busy. (*Beat.*) I hope you're havin' a good time.' I said 'Well, actually I'm at home – watchin' Jools Holland (*Beat.*) – havin' a glass of wine,' He said – 'Are you not goin' out anywhere?' An' I said 'Well, I've no one special.' (*Beat.*) 'E text back an' said – '*I'd* like to be your "someone special".' (*Beat.*) But 'e said 'I really, *really* would like to take you out – to lunch – I'd really like to, take you out – an' see you with your clothes on.' (*She laughs.*)

Ah – an' then from there we've been seeing each other every weekend. (*Pause.*) But it has really bowled me over, it's kind of like – an' 'e just makes me laugh, so much. (*Beat.*) An' he is just so generous of heart – not just of money. (*Beat.*) Y'know an' I'm just not *used* to that kind of attention. / (*The phone rings. Beat.*) You know – I am truly *pampered*.

POPPY. No.

TESSA *continues to struggle with the flat-pack.*

Pause.

SUZIE. I met some of his friends last weekend (*Beat.*) – which was really nice. (*Beat.*) I am the *girl*friend. Yeah (*Beat.*) – I am the girlfriend. (*Beat.*) Seee, 'e, 'e bought me this – uh-also, on Monday, got this – and 'e knows where I put my keys, an' 'e put this on my key / – without me knowing –

POPPY. Oh, my Go-[d] – I need someone like that, I / *do* –

SUZIE. – an' I picked up my keys I was like – 'Oh my *God*!' (*Beat.*) I said 'You just – did you just do that?' (*Beat.*) 'Yeah.' (*Beat.*) Was like 'Ooh!' (*Beat, then she giggles.*)

Pause.

He's got me on the *car* insurance fer 'is Pamph- – 'is, uum (*Beat.*) – Ford (*Beat.*) – Panther –

TESSA. Oo-oh! / (*Beat.*) Yer in there, girl.

SUZIE. So that's good, that's a good sign.

Beat.

TESSA. Yer – (*Softly.*) it's love. (*Beat.*) / Innit sickening?

SUZIE. It's a good sign. It's quite serious, already. (*Beat.*) Well he's already declared that he loves me. (*Beat.*) He's taking me away – An' I know, an' I've never been (*Beat.*) – nobody's ever taken me away – for Valentine's. I been countin' down the days all week.

Beat.

TESSA. Oh, dunnit make you *sick* –

POPPY. Yeah, it does actually, yeah.

The phone rings. TESSA *gets up quickly to answer it, hoping it will be the phantom caller as she has decided how to pay him back.*

TESSA. Hello can I help you?

The call is for SUZIE *instead so* TESSA *passes her the phone.*

SUZIE. He-*llo*? (*Beat.*) Yes it *is*, good afternoon. (*Pause. A slight giggle.*) I'm based in Wednes- on Wednesday I'm in *Bourne*mouth, and every other day of the week I'm in Christchurch – very passionate lady, offers the full Girlfriend Experience, I enjoy lots of kissing, cuddling oral *both* ways – I do do oral with*out*, but not to completion, and I don't do anything pain-related, purely a pleasure lady (*Beat.*) All right sweet'art, see you at four. (*Beat.*) Bye.

She hangs up the phone. Pause.

(*To audience.*) The Girlfriend Experience. (*To* POPPY.) What do you consider to be the Girlfriend Experience?

POPPY. Erm. Mmm. Well it seems like it's more personal. Ya know. It's like / uhm – more kissing cuddling (*Beat.*) –

SUZIE. More intimate.

POPPY. – talking. I dunno. Just more passio-[nate] – not raunchy. Yeah, / yeah no like that whole thing –

SUZIE. See the raunchy. Have you heard of the Porn-Star Experience? (*Beat.*) Some girls offer the Porn-Star Experience which is they drag them into the bedroom and it's – you're at it / straight away an' it's all very –

POPPY. Yeah,

SUZIE. – like a porn film. (*Matter-of-fact.*) 'Oh yeah baby.' Ya know. 'Fuck me harder' an' ya know an' it's all very full-on. Whereas ours is a – is a more kindof a caring sharing (*Beat.*) – kindof a – a service.

Pause.

So your plan still going ahead to g- – move in 'ere?

TESSA. Yes – yeah –

Beat.

SUZIE. How hairy is Sam? (*Beat.*) I was jus' cuz you know I've got an allergy to dogs. (*Beat.*) But I can take – Benadryl (*Beat.*) – but I would / have to, I won't kiss 'im –

TESSA.Well we won't get 'im anywhere *near* you.

Beat.

SUZIE (*sniffs*). Tha's all right then. (*Sniffs.*) But I jus' thought I'd warn you. (*Beat.*) Do you think you're gonna cope?

TESSA. Oh yeah cuz it's so cut off and Becky's got her transport all sorted out for school – erm – on the seafront.

SUZIE. It's all coming together.

TESSA. Oh yeah.

Pause.

The phone rings. TESSA *answers it.*

He-llo, can I help you? (*Beat.*) Ooh, just in *ti-iiiime*. (*Pause.*) You ready?

She plays 'Bad Things' by Wednesday 13 into the phone at full volume on her CD player.

Scene Three – Valentine's Special

Late afternoon. 14th February 2007. POPPY *and* TESSA *are watching* The Pirates of the Caribbean. POPPY *is wearing a wig, bright purple with pigtails.* TESSA *is wearing a red, shoulder-length wig with a Gestapo hat on top. She is scoffing Cadbury's Mini Eggs.*

Long pause as the women watch the film.

POPPY. Zat the door? (*She burps.*) Pardon me. (*Beat.*) Can I 'ave my other Red Bull in a minute? (*Pause.*) Tessa.

Beat.

TESSA. Hm?

POPPY *laughs.*

Sorry?

POPPY. Can I 'ave my other Red Bull in a minute / (*Beat.*) – please –

TESSA. Yeah.

Pause.

(*Mimicking the television.*) 'O-oh!'

Pause. As TESSA *gets the Red Bull, we can hear Johnny Depp on the television.* TESSA *shuts the fridge. She chuckles.*

POPPY. Thank you.

Pause.

TESSA. Oh I talked to Suzie, last night (*Beat.*) – oh she left last night (*Beat.*) – an' she went – on the Blue-bell – Railway is it? (*Beat.*) / Bluebell Railway –

POPPY. Oh, yeah.

TESSA. I was li-[ke], says 'I's been *pissin'* down wi' rain – '

POPPY *chuckles.*

'Oh, it don't matter.' I thought, 'Oh, God, you gorra be in love,' int you, you know. (*Beat.*) To be *rained* on and don't *care.*

They laugh.

POPPY. It's romantic.

TESSA. I said 'Oh, for the *love* of *God*!' (*Beat.*) I said 'Oh, have a nice time.' (*High-pitched voice.*) 'Ooh-yeah we just – (*Lower pitch, sultry voice.*) we're just gonna (*Beat.*) – we're just getting ready to go down to dinner.

She hoots, then again after a beat.

In this big four, *five*-star (*Beat.*) – hotel.'

POPPY. Mm.

TESSA. Oh, yeah. Bitch – hate 'er.

She laughs.

A lull. They watch television for a while.

Oh well (*Beat.*) – oh, *Mork*!

She picks up Mork, her favourite teddy and cuddles it tightly.

Mork Mork, Mork. (*Pause. High-pitched squeal.*) Mork.

POPPY *giggles.*

(*A sigh.*) Haahh (*Beat.*) – don't ya just *love* teddies?

Pause.

POPPY. Yeah, see, now an' again – see, this is the thing with Suzie – now an' again it's nice (*Beat.*) – you know – could do with a bit of that now an' again –

TESSA. Ooh, yeah / (*Beat.*) – yeah –

POPPY. Yeah.

TESSA. Yeah.

Another lull.

The phone rings and TESSA *answers it.*

(*Putting on a snooty accent.*) He-llo, can I help you? (*Beat.*) Na-na-na-no, everything's for half an hour (*Beat.*) – uum, it's, uh – forty is fer a nice massage (*Beat.*) – uh, either hand or breast relief. (*Beat.*) Uuh, fifty is either straight sex an' a massage, *or* – oral without – um – uh, an' a nice massage (*Beat.*) – and sixty, basically is a bit of everythink. (*Beat.*) But it's – but it's all half an hour, no matter *what.* (*Pause.*) Okay sweetheart (*Beat.*) – ba-bye.

She puts down the phone.

(*Mimicking a high-pitched man's voice.*) 'I rang earlier –

POPPY *laughs.*

– do you base your (*Beat.*) – do you base your prices on (*Beat.*) – *services*, or – or how *long*?' (*Beat.*) I said 'No everything's, *fuckin'* half-hour.' (*Puts on his voice again.*) 'Oh-ooh (*Beat.*) – oh I'm a bit confused – ' (*Beat.*) Wha's ta be, *confused* about?

Pause.

Valentine's – special. (*Beat.*) We're the cheapest in town, (*Pause as she scoffs some Mini Eggs.*) – no hidden extras, so – cheapest in fuckin' town, an' 'e wants us to do a Valentine's special. (*Beat.*) Piss off.

POPPY *laughs*.

Pause.

The doorbell rings. TESSA *gets up and goes to answer it.*

MIKE (*off*). Hi / (*Beat*.) – how's you?

TESSA (*off*). Hel-*looo*. (*Beat*.) I'm fine. (*She giggles*.)

MIKE *chuckles*.

MIKE (*off*). Good.

TESSA *giggles*.

TESSA (*off*). You're looking very, dapper – / today –

MIKE. (*off*) That's very kind of you / – thank you.

TESSA (*off*). Mmm. (*Beat*.) In the room (*Beat*.) – go – / now –

MIKE *chuckles*. TESSA *giggles*. *They go towards the bedroom*.

Excuse the wild comb. Went out, got wet. (*She laughs*.)

MIKE. I know. / Brutal out there, isn't it?

TESSA. So um. Moi or would you like to see Poppy or (*Beat*.) – someone else or no chance sorry. Hah ha, you don't have the choice.

TESSA *laughs naughtily and comes back into the sitting room to put away his money*.

(*Whispering*.) This is *Mike*. *Ooo – ooh – ooh!*

POPPY. Have I got to say – hello, or is 'e yours?

TESSA. No s'*mine*.

POPPY *continues watching the film briefly, and* TESSA *is heading to the bedroom, when the doorbell rings again*. POPPY *gets up to answer it*.

Oh fuck. I'm ever so sorry. 'The room's not ready', you'll have to say. Another twen'y before –

POPPY. Well half an hour it's gonna be innit? Yeah. What time is it now?

Beat.

TESSA. Three.

POPPY (*very quietly*). Awright.

She opens the front door.

Hia –

GROPER. Hi/a.

POPPY. Uuummm (*Beat.*) – nobody available for half an hour, cuz we've on'y got one room – um. Err, if you'd like to / come back in half an hour –

GROPER (*to* TESSA *as she passes into the bedroom with* MIKE). Hi.

POPPY. – is that all right?

GROPER. About half an hour? / What's the time now?

POPPY. Yeah – just over. Uhm. I think that's right. *So* say about –

GROPER. Are you P-

POPPY. I'm Poppy yeah.

GROPER. I've heard about you, ya know.

POPPY. Oh thank you. / Well I hope it's all good.

GROPER. Yeah.

She laughs.

So you're, you're actually busy are you?

POPPY. Tessa's busy. Uhm the other room's not ready so that's why we're only using one room.

GROPER. Uhm (*Pause.*) – cuz it means I've gotta basically I've got to hang around. Uhm –

Pause.

POPPY (*gently laughing*). Sorry. I mean she – ya know it's her place. / She said there's no –

GROPER. Yeah.

POPPY. – there are no other rooms ready.

GROPER. So there's no – no rooms?

POPPY. She's got an appointment now so it'll be like half hour.

Beat.

GROPER. Mmmm – all right I'll try an' come back.

POPPY. All right, okay.

GROPER. What do you uhm (*Beat.*) – what do you charge normally?

POPPY. Ahhh-mmmm (*Beat.*) – sixty for, half an hour. Again I don't have any extras. The only thing I do ext-[ra] – would charge extra for is anal. I don't know if you're (*Beat.*) into that? / (*She laughs.*)

GROPER. Mm-hmm. (*Beat.*) You are obviously.

POPPY. Yeah.

Pause.

GROPER. So say you just wanted straight sex, do you do it with a Durex?

POPPY. Yeah.

GROPER. You don't do it without?

POPPY. Nn-no.

GROPER. Never?

POPPY. N-no.

GROPER (*half-laughing*). Can't be tempted?

POPPY. Uummm (*Pause.*) – *poss*ibly.

GROPER. Yeah?

POPPY. Possibly but obviously, not (*Beat.*) – ya know, to completion.

GROPER. What can you have it up but get it out before / I cum?

POPPY. Yeah. Yes. Yeah. (*Beat.*) But really I don't do that, cuz I've only done that once before an' it's not a good thing to get into, really. Uhm. (*Beat.*) I'd have to think about that. But do you want my number / anyway?

GROPER. Yeah. Can you write it down for me?

POPPY. Okay come in for just a second then –

GROPER *closes the front door behind him and walks down the hallway towards the sitting room.*

GROPER. Shall I just follow you in there?

POPPY. Yeah, just stay –

POPPY *enters the sitting room, writes her number down on a scrap of paper, and goes back out to the hallway.*

There you go.

GROPER. You – you do it up yer arse with a Durex don't you?

POPPY. Yes.

GROPER. You don't do it without up there?

POPPY. No that's more sort of a diseasy / thing –

GROPER. Yeah.

POPPY. – but obviously (*Beat.*) – cuz I'm not actually on any other contraception at the moment, so it'd be equally bad –

GROPER. No.

POPPY. – you'd 'ave to be very very safe.

GROPER. But you could do it – an' pull it out as it's cummin' – yeah?

POPPY. Yeah, if you're goo-[d] – if you're –

POPPY *laughs.*

GROPER (*tuneful hum*). Hmm-hm-/hmmm –

POPPY. – *reliable* at that, / sorta thing – or –

GROPER. – yeahhh. (*Beat.*) Erm. (*Beat.*) Do you shave?

POPPY. I – do, but – I'm not really, at the moment.

GROPER. It's nice and bushy is it? (*Beat.*) *Yeah.* Let's 'ave a look.

POPPY *lifts up her negligee to show him.*

POPPY. S'a bit, I mean – I-I shave round here (*Beat.*) – and here.

Beat.

GROPER. / Mmm –

POPPY. / – that's enough.

GROPER. Coo. I'd like to put my cock in that. Feel that cock.

POPPY *giggles*.

Corr. That was nice seein' that.

POPPY *laughs*.

Show me your nipples before I go then.

POPPY *sighs*.

She does so. At this point and he starts to fondle her.

GROPER. Corr. Zat nice?

POPPY. Yeah – s'nice.

GROPER (*pointing to bathroom*). Can't we just stand in there?

POPPY (*whispering*). No!

GROPER. She won't know.

POPPY. No, honestly (*Beat.*) – that's enough –

GROPER. Eh?

POPPY. – that's enough now / now –

GROPER. Look I got a johnny.

POPPY. No.

GROPER. No?

POPPY. Sorry. (*Beat.*) No-ah! (*Beat.*) No, come on –

GROPER. Please.

POPPY. – come on. (*Beat.*) There's limits, there's limits there's limits. Come on.

POPPY *giggles*.

Gotta / be strict –

GROPER. Eh? (*Beat.*) I reckon I might be back in half an hour.

POPPY. All right then. (*Laughs.*)

Pause.

(*Sighs*.) Come on. I'm gonna see you out. I got things to do.

GROPER. No. All right. Corr, that was nice ya know? (*Beat*.) Eh? I got that horny. / Just put it up there –

POPPY *laughs softly*.

– I always fancied standin' up in a bathroom doin' it, ya see.

POPPY. Oh, all right.

Beat.

GROPER. Nice doin' it.

POPPY *laughs gently*.

See ya soon.

POPPY (*forced laugh*). Bye.

GROPER. Bye.

The door slams.

Beat.

POPPY. Oh my *God*. (*Beat*.) Oh my *God*, get a*way* from him!

We hear TESSA *orgasming*.

POPPY *re-enters the sitting room, sits down and lights a cigarette. 'The Shoop Shoop Song (It's in his Kiss)' is playing on the television, she sings along sardonically*.

'It's in his his kiss', yeah right.

Beat. We hear TESSA *giggling inside the bedroom*.

TESSA *laughs. A playful slap is heard*.

TESSA (*off*). Stop it! (*Laughs. Beat*.) Okay, I'm gonna let ya go.

Pause. TESSA *starts to come back in*.

Hmmm. Right. (*Beat. A sigh*.) Hah. (*Beat*.) What do ya think?

TESSA *chuckles*. MIKE *joins in*.

See you. (*Beat*.) Okay – I'll, uh (*Beat*.) – text you –

MIKE. Yeah.

They kiss.

TESSA. Bye!

MIKE. Ba-bye.

TESSA. Yes – go!

They both giggle.

The door shuts. Beat.

TESSA *starts walking down the hallway into the sitting room.*

(*Softly, to herself.*) Yes! (*Beat. Louder, orgasmic.*) Yes, yes *yes*! (*Beat. A hoot.*) Hoo-hoo-hoo! (*Giggles.*) Um-hah – mmm. (*She hums absently, then giggles.*)

TESSA *enters the sitting room, unable to contain herself.*

POPPY. Oh yeah?

TESSA (*laughs*). I've got a *date*! (*Laughs.*)

POPPY. A *date*?

TESSA (*giggles*). Y-*yeah*!

TESSA*'s voice rises into a noise of excitement and happiness.*

Not this Friday next *Fri*day. (*Beat. A hoot.*) Hoo-*hoo*!

POPPY. Fuck's sake. I'm just ya know – duh-duh-duh-durrrr –

TESSA. Fuckin' *hell*! (*Beat.*) Fuckin', *heeell*! (*Beat. Whispering.*) I've never done that (*Beat.*) – *ever*. Aw, fuck, what've I *done*?

TESSA *laughs, getting louder and more excited. Claps her hands together.*

Scene Four – Dirty Old Men

Midday. 13th April 2007. TESSA *has now moved in entirely with her daughter. There are unpacked boxes scattered in the sitting room and hallway.* TESSA *is clearly stressed and does her best to organise the chaos. A messy but more homely feel. Sam,* TESSA's *dog, is barking.*

TESSA. Sam it's a *car*! Shut *up*! (*Sam barks again.*) – Give it a rest, now.

More barking. TESSA *goes into the kitchen.*

(*Shouting over barking.*) Sam! (*Beat.*) Right, that's *it*. Samuel! You get! Back up. Don't get fucking sweet and innocent with me.

SUZIE. Don't – eyeball the dog. (*Beat.*) 'E's – 'e's *nice* doggie, but – 'e'sa workin' dog, so don't eyeball 'im. (*Beat.*) Don't talk to 'im.

A dog-toy squeaks. The phone rings.

TESSA. Hello can I help you? (*Beat.*) Oh! Well she's busy at the moment. She'll be about five minutes or so.

AMBER *enters.*

Ahh! Oh. She's here – she's here. Here she is.

TESSA *passes* AMBER *the phone.*

It's your beloved. I was havin' a chat.

AMBER. Oh were you? (*On the phone.*) Oh, right. O-kay. (*Beat.*) Okay, yeah I bought six, fer one ninety-nine or summink – awright then? You alright though? (*Beat.*) Oh, cool – cool. (*Beat.*) Tha's right – yeah (*Beat.*) – we're havin' (*Beat.*) – we're havin' a weekend to our*selves* (*Beat,* TESSA *starts laughing.*) – yes, cool / – that's all right then –

TESSA. You'll be lucky.

AMBER. Alright. I got you a Mars Bar. (*Beat.*) I won't eat y- I won't eat your Mars Bar. Right – I'm going now on that note.

Cuz you're picking on me again. (*Beat.*) Oh you have a marriage contract do you?

Pause.

I see. Okay (*Beat.*) – ha'n't stopped for the last *hour*. (*Beat.*) She gives me all the decrepit ones. / Right, I'm, on that note I'm goin'. (*Beat.*) Cuz, I need a smoke, now. (*Beat.*) Is that all right? (*Pause.*) I love you too. See you. Fank you for ringing me. Bye bye.

TESSA. Yeah!

SUZIE. I bought me nurse's uniform today, I thought I might dress up it I in just *feel* like dressing up today, I don't know what's wrong wi' me. (*Beat.*) / Felt like somink diff- different, on.

TESSA. Oo-*ar*.

AMBER. And why not.

TESSA. You're in a dressy-up mood / – aren't you.

SUZIE. I am in a dressy-up mood today.

TESSA. Oh. (*Beat.*) Oh there's stuff everywhere, still (*Beat.*) – cuz 'e hasn't put the shelves up, so, *yep*! (*Beat. To Sam in the kitchen.*) Over there (*Beat.*) – and, um (*Beat.*) – mm, Becky's room we 'aven't been able to use for two days. (*Beat. Laughing.*) Because it's just 'ad everything stuffed in there.

AMBER. Oh it's a nuthouse, it's not a whorehouse, it's a nuthouse.

Beat. TESSA *gets a text.*

TESSA. Oh look, Mike – yes. (*Beat. She reads the text.*) 'Hi sexy, very horny for *you*.' (*Beat. Sighs.*) / Fuck, *off.*

SUZIE. Tell 'im – tell 'im –

TESSA. Just go – away (*Beat.*) – just, go (*Beat.*) – leave me – the fuck alone – I'm, not interested, any more. (*Beat.*) We went out on the Wednes-, was it Wednesday?

AMBER. Yes.

TESSA. Goes out (*Beat.*) – aan', uhhh – both a you, Poppy *was* right, we went to, fucking Clapgate Common – yeah (*Beat.*) – / so we've –

SUZIE. So 'e was after some car fun?

TESSA. Yeah.

Beat.

SUZIE. Wha' *dogging* car fun?

TESSA. Yeah.

SUZIE. Right okay.

TESSA. *So* – we gets up there, it's, pissin' down with rain (*Beat.*) – we did it – two or three times (*Beat.*) – in two hours, tha's not bad, / is it?

SUZIE. Oh that's not bad – at / all –

TESSA. Errr –

They both laugh.

SUZIE. In a *car*!

TESSA. In a car.

SUZIE *laughs.*

Hey, at least it weren't a Mini – y'know what I mean? (*Beat.*) An' 'e's goin', 'Oh, yeah,' ya know, 'it's not just the *sex*, I'd like to take you *out.*' (*Beat.*) Uh – you know, 'We'll do it, uh – a-at, *your* pace,' cuz I'm sayin', 'Look – '

SUZIE. Mmm.

TESSA. – you know, 'this is, sorta – taboo ground for me (*Beat.*) – ya know, I wanna bit a *fun*, I don't want-t to *go* anywhere, blahblah*blah* – ' (*Beat.*) I said s-then, uh – 'Well, you know, do it at *my* speed.' (*Beat.*) He's, 'Oh, no-no-no – that's cool, tha's, that's *fine.*' (*Beat.*) Heee, dropped me back off we got back about quar'er past twe'y past midnight (*Beat.*) – he's sayin' all this, you know, 'Ooh, we'll take our time – you text me when you're ready, blahblah-blah.' (*Beat.*) I 'adn't got through the *door*, within half an hour it's like (*Pause.*) – 'Oh, that was fuckin' fantastic, ne-[ed] – you know, w-want *more.*' (*Pause.*) This is leavin' it, you know this is – uh-uh-urrr (*Beat.*) – an' I thought, 'Ohh, I'm too tired now I'm goin' *bed.*' (*Pause.*) So, next day – 'Mornin' sexy' (*Beat.*) – urrrm, 'Want some more car sex, with *you.*'

SUZIE. No.

TESSA. – uh, eh – This is leavin' me alone, ta, do it in *my* time? (*Beat.*) Mm? (*Beat.*) An' it's been like that, / ever – since.

49

SUZIE. Too pushy.

Beat.

SUZIE *receives a text message.*

SUZIE. Derek's just, left me a song at home – said 'I've left you a song on your – on your home phone.' (*Beat.*) Sung me a song, 'e said 'I've left it on your home answerphone.' (*Beat.*) We are now, joint members together, of Na-, of the National Trust, so it must be – / love –

TESSA. Oh, my *God* –

SUZIE. I said 'You can't dump me for a year, now' – I said 'cuz we're joint members of National Trust.' (*Beat.*) Bit – serious. / (*Laughs.*)

TESSA. Ooo-er, ooo-er. (*Beat.*) Makes ya *sick*, dun' it, eh – makes ya ss-*sick*.

The doorbell rings.

Oh for fuck's sake. I'll go shall I?

SUZIE. Yes Tessa, 'sabout time you did something.

AMBER. I'm glad you said that.

TESSA *goes to answer the door. She shows the punter,* GLOVE MAN, *into a bedroom, shuts the door to talk him through the prices and services.*

SUZIE. It's good to see tha you're well.

AMBER. Yes. I'm feelin so much better / I was a pain in the *butt* with it, an' I know I was but –

SUZIE. You could tell in your face you were –

AMBER. – phew –

SUZIE. You're / okay now.

AMBER. Gone.

SUZIE. Gone.

AMBER. Gone. (*Beat.*) But I'm not going NHS ever again. / Goin' private next time –

SUZIE. No?

AMBER. – not bein' treated like a –

SUZIE. I heard you got your gallstone. So yeah I find out
Wednesday about Dad an' chemo an' stuff – what they'll say. I
don't think they'll start it.

AMBER. I'd be very very / surprised. He's too weak still – no cuz
it's gonna knock him for *six* (*Beat.*) – Yeah. (*Beat.*) It's not
good.

SUZIE. No. He's not strong enough. He's not strong enough.

TESSA *re-enters the sitting room.*

TESSA (*whispering*). He's an old – aged pensioner. (*Beat.*) 'E's got
prostate trouble – 'e just wants *workin'* off –

AMBER *laughs.*

His flies are all – (*Beat. Louder.*) Go an' say 'ello.

SUZIE *exits to the bedroom and shuts the door behind.*

(*Mock-crying.*) Please don't choose, me. (*Beat.*) I'm busy!

AMBER. Me too –

Pause.

SUZIE *re-enters.*

SUZIE. His name's – Hector –

AMBER. Oh, fuck –

SUZIE. An' 'e went – he's given me the same story –

AMBER. Oh well I / get –

SUZIE. Did he mention leather gloves to you?

TESSA. No –

AMBER. Oh, that was the / one I 'ad on the *phone*.

AMBER *exits to the bedroom and closes the door.*

SUZIE. He's (*Beat.*) – he's got leather gloves. He jus' wants to be
wanked off with leather gloves. (*Beat. Whispering.*) He's got a
wonky eye. He's got leather gloves himself.

TESSA. Oh – I was gonna say. Okay. I was gonna say I've got leather gloves.

Pause.

SUZIE. I bet he chooses Amber.

TESSA. I bet –

AMBER *re-enters and points at* TESSA, *indicating that* GLOVE MAN *has chosen her.*

(*Whispering.*) Oh no – *nooo*!

AMBER (*laughing*). Yeah –

They're all laughing, sniggering as quietly as they can.

TESSA. Aw, fuck – off – fuck – off!

They're all trying to suppress the sniggers.

– *Fuck!*

AMBER. Get in there.

More laughter as they start to lace TESSA *into the leather gloves.*

TESSA (*through sniggers*). Shit!

They're still lacing her.

AMBER. That's – it.

TESSA.Yeah.

SUZIE. 'Ang on – 'ang on –

More lacing.

TESSA. They do stretch. (*Beat.*) That's it –

SUZIE (*whispering*). It's like dressing the mistress.

AMBER (*laughing*). The mistress is very –

SUZIE. Do you want some talc on with them?

TESSA. No.

SUZIE. Just have one on.

TESSA. Hang on – no he wants both.

SUZIE. It'll take him an hour to get undressed anyway. (*Pause.*) I noticed his flies were already undone.

TESSA. I know he came in with it like that. (*Clears her throat. Beat. Whispering.*) Okay. Yeah. That's it.

SUZIE (*whispering*). Zat tight, too / tight?

TESSA. Yeah. No, that's cool – hm.

TESSA *takes a deep breath.*

SUZIE (*whispering*). Okay mistress –

TESSA *lets out her breath in a half-laugh.*

AMBER. Away you go.

Beat.

TESSA. I'll get you.

They laugh quietly.

Beat.

Sam barks.

(*Shouting.*) Shut up!

Sam barks.

SUZIE. This couple – who I know (*Beat.*) – I actually told 'em on Monday, that I'm an escort. (*Beat.*) They were fi-[ne] absolutely fine, about it. (*Beat.*) Ah no they're just intrigued, about how I got, in to it, stuff, an', like the question, he said to me – 'How'd'you cope' – he said, 'if-if you – if you (*Beat.*) – if there's a *guy*, who you jus' don't fancy – or, he's too *old*, or he's – *ugly*, or – ' (*Beat.*) Ya'[kn]ow, an' I said – 'Well (*Beat.*) – uumm, you know – I just *see* through that (*Beat.*) – I see through that to the person they are, they've got needs (*Beat.*) – an' I – put myself – in the role of a *carer*.' I said (*Beat.*) – 'An' *some* guys, who I've thought, "Hmm – *no*",' I said, 'have been fan*tas*tic lovers.' (*Beat.*) You know, it's taught me a lesson 'bout not judging people, by their looks. (*Beat.*) An' I had this dis-abled guy on Sunday – an' he's, um (*Beat.*) – got a prosthetic leg, his rr-, he's lost his right, leg, err – a-at the knee (*Beat.*) – aand, he's got – he's had quite extensive abdominal surgery, as well (*Beat.*) – an' he's had leg ulcers and things on his *right* le-[g], his *left* leg, so 'e doesn't look, absolutely fantast-[ic]. (*Beat.*) Lo-[ve], he had the most, lovely eyes (*Beat.*) – he'd had, um, problem – h-he'd had recent surgery (*Beat.*) – an' I just had to be careful, of where I touched, an' stuff – but (*Beat.*) – he had the most lovely smile – an' the most lovely eyes – that you just, I – you know, at the end – I just didn't realise he wo- he only had one leg. (*Beat.*) You know, an' I was saying to this guy – Paul, I said – 'The only thing I think, I – I, *personally* couldn't *cope* with (*Beat.*) – is a colostomy bag.' (*Pause.*) He said 'No no, I can understand that.' (*Beat.*) I said 'Because – it's (*Beat.*) – bodily, waste, an' – is involved, an', – I said 'I just – don't think ma – I got a weak stomach.' (*Beat. Laughs.*) Really don't think I could do it. (*Beat.*) I mean, part of the role, is that (*Beat.*) – you do, be-*come* (*Beat.*) – a sex-therapist-stroke-counsellor (*Beat.*) – to a lot of people.

Spanking can be heard coming from the bedroom.

AMBER. Think she's 'avin' a bit of a hard time in there.

SUZIE. Mm. (*Beat.*) Oh God. Hope she's chargin' 'im more than for'y quid.

Pause. The phone rings and AMBER *answers it.*

AMBER. He-llo can I *help* you? (*Pause.*) Hello Becky (*Beat.*) – it's me. How are you? (*Beat.*) Oh (*Beat.*) – ah-you want to know when to come down, don't you? (*Beat.*) Um – well your mum's busy at the moment, I fink she said after eight, ish? (*Pause.*) Yeah. (*Pause.*) Make it *after* eight. (*Beat.*) Ah, all right then. (*Beat.*) See ya later – take care, bye!

Pause.

The phone rings again. SUZIE *answers it.*

SUZIE (*coughs*). Hello (*Beat.*) – I'll let her know, and who shall I say'll be calling? (*Beat.*) Jim?

She hangs up.

AMBER. That's Viagra Man, / that's Viagra Man.

SUZIE. Okay, I'll let her know, okay, bye. Thought I recognised his voice.

AMBER. That's Viagra Man, Jim.

Sam barks. TESSA *and* GLOVE MAN *come out of the bedroom.*

(*Whispering loudly.*) Sam! / Shut up!

TESSA. Shush.

Sam barks again.

Shush.

Sam keeps barking over their conversation.

GLOVE MAN. What's yer dog called?

TESSA. Springer spaniel. (*Beat.*) English.

GLOVE MAN. Ha ha. Brenda? (*Beat. Gently laughing.*) I've got a-a girl – friend named Brenda not a cocker spaniel.

TESSA *laughs.*

TESSA. Shush now – noisy.

AMBER (*whispering*). Sam, / shut up.

Sam barks, and then again. TESSA *is laughing softly.*

TESSA (*laughing*). You watch how you're doing – have a lovely time, thank you.

She kisses him.

M-wah.

GLOVE MAN. Thank you my love.

TESSA (*kisses him*). Mm-wah.

GLOVE MAN. I, have enjoyed it, so much.

TESSA (*giggling*). Cool! (*Beat.*) You take care.

GLOVE MAN. You too.

TESSA. Watch how you go up the steps.

GLOVE MAN. Yeah, I will I-I –

TESSA. Be careful.

Beat.

GLOVE MAN. I like the smack of your pads on my bare arse.

TESSA *gives a dirty giggle*. HECTOR *joins in*.

TESSA (*still giggling*). You, naughty! (*Beat, giggling*.) Go on, away / with ya.

GLOVE MAN. *I am* naughty!

TESSA. A-*way* with you.

TESSA *giggles*.

GLOVE MAN (*off*). Look out for that dog whip?

TESSA. Ooh – no. (*Giggles*.) He doesn't like people.

GLOVE MAN (*off*). What?

TESSA. He doesn't like people. (*Beat*.) He doesn't *like* people.

GLOVE MAN (*off*). The dog whip!

TESSA. Oh the dog – oh, I thought you meant the dog! (*Laughs*.) I certainly will.

GLOVE MAN (*off*). O-kay.

Beat.

TESSA. Oh! (*Beat*.) Jesus Christ.

Beat.

SUZIE. Was 'e all right? (*Beat*.) I hope you charged 'im more'n forty quid?

Beat.

TESSA. Naaahh.

SUZIE. Uum, uh you got an appointment at half past four –

TESSA. Oh. (*Beat*.) Not another one. (*Beat*.) Not one of (*Beat*.) – / those.

AMBER. Erp (*Beat*.) – uh-oh.

SUZIE. Ss – Jim.

TESSA. Jim.

Beat. AMBER *bursts into raucous laughter*.

Viagra man.

AMBER *bursts into laughter again*.

Scene Five – Reality Check

Early afternoon. 18th July 2007. TESSA *is lying on the sofa watching Jeremy Kyle, whilst nursing a bottle of Jameson's. She is half-ready for work.*

TESSA. This past – few weeks (*Beat.*) – I mean, we closed for three days. (*Beat.*) Oooh. (*Beat.*) Oh, I was gonna – stop everything. I'm looking through the paper looking for a fucking job. Bad. (*Beat.*) I needed a break. (*Beat.*) Just with everything, with Mike, with these dirty old men. Ohh, I just couldn't handle it. It was like 'wooh' put the barriers up quick. (*Laughs.*) Things are changing for me every single day something is changing within me and without.

Pause.

It's – I dunno, p'raps it's comin' to the r-realistic thing, of – uuhh – coming up to *sixty* (*Beat.*) – um, er – p'raaaps realising, that – uumm (*Beat.*) – this is it. (*Beat.*) This is my life – an' that there isn't gonna be anybody – else (*Beat.*) – so I've got to hold on to the reins. (*Beat.*) There is me and me alone. It's, it's having no one just me (*Beat.*) – and obviously the children. An' the more I *accept* things (*Beat.*) – for the way they are, an' look at the *reality* of it (*Beat.*) – I can separate fantasy (*Beat.*) – from reality. (*Beat.*) That somebody *was* going to come into my life, somebody – you know, I-I'm, gonna bump into, an' it's gonna be all roses round the door an' *what*ever (*Beat.*) – uhhh – the Mills 'n' *Boon* – thing (*Beat.*) – which is still there, that is – *that* is the fantasy. (*Beat.*) But I can, separate it from reality – cuz (*Beat.*) – it's not *happening* (*Beat.*) – it never *has* 'appened.

Pause. Sighs.

Triumphantly she downs the last of the Jameson's.

W-when we go an' see this play – I don't know whether I *can* or not (*Beat.*) – to be *quite* honest – looking at me (*Beat.*) – an' list'ning to *me* (*Beat.*) – and to what *I* actually *say*, the fuckin' verbal diarrhea that comes outta my *mouth* (*Beat.*) – uh, i-it's quite frightening. (*Beat.*) Cuz it *is*, *me*! (*Beat.*) But that's 'ow – that's 'ow I, I wannit to *be*, because it's showing that, that, it – that we *are* real. (*Beat.*) An', hopefully, people w-will appreciate that we're not all crackheads, an', an' – an', you know w-what we're *painted* as, what these people like Jerry (*Beat*.) – Jeremy Kyle (*Beat*.) – you were, you know, you say the word 'prositute' 'Oh so you're *scum*' – you know, 'you've wasted your *life*, you're – y'you know, you're *noth-ing*, you could be *bet*-ter, you could be-' (*Beat*.) *No*. (*Beat*.) You know, I'm, I-I'm – I'm okay with it, I'm, I'm good at what I *do*. It's a *job*, for God's sake, so gettin' *that across*, is maybe *worth*, going through the – (*Gasps, a nervous, excited sound*.) Woo-ooo cringe-factor.(*Pause. A heavy sigh*.)

She gets up and starts lacing her boots.

I got another one today, who's coming, at half past *three* – this John, who I'm gonna turn down *completely*, cuz I've thought about it – and thought for what 'e pays, I don't wanna see 'im cuz 'e's, fuckin' arsehole (*Beat*.) – so 'e c'n piss *off*. (*Beat*.) 'E-'e tries to pay *thirty* quid – an' 'e wants *every*thing for nothing – he's there for ever, 'yakyakyakyakyak' – an' he's just a ts-dis*gust*ing, old – dirty filthy old man. Very abrasive on these. (*Indicating her chest*.) He just repulses me and I'm thinking do I really need the money that badly? No, I don't.

Pause. POPPY *enters.*

POPPY. Could you put that in the, fridge for me / (*Beat*.) – please.

TESSA. No.

POPPY. I 'aven't drunk since Saturday night, aren't I / good?

TESSA. God aren't *you* bloody good.

Beat.

POPPY. *Actually* I've decided now – yesterday – I *love* my body – I'm going to treat it better. (*Beat*.) Which means – cuttin' down on the booze (*Beat*.) – cuttin' out, well, cuttin' down on the fags / (*Beat*.) – cuz –

TESSA. Ooh!

POPPY. I *know* – so –

TESSA. Ooo-ooooh!

POPPY. – I was layin' in (*Beat*.) – laid in bed, last night, an' thinkin', 'Mm – mmm (*Beat*.) – that's all right.' (*Giggles. Laughing*.) It's / (*Beat*.) – fine –

TESSA. I'm lyin' in bed last night, going 'What the fuck're you *doin'*, Tessa –

POPPY *laughs*.

– you got every fuckin' opportunity to *do* this, why aren't you *doing* it?

POPPY*'s laughter trails off*.

I'll jus' get up an' have another – Jack Daniels.' (*Beat. Sighs*.) Yesterday, I 'ad a bo'le a wine (*Beat*.) – an', err – I bought a Jameson's, I drank half of that, this isn't ee- the other *half* –

Beat.

POPPY. Yerr.

TESSA. – wha' am I *doin'*?

Beat.

POPPY. Oh, I've been like that, / though –

TESSA. *What* – am I do-, uh-eh-oh (*Beat*.) – you know? (*Beat*.) I'm, fuckin' *killin'* myself, I know I am. (*Suddenly remembering*.) Oh! / (*Beat*.) Bad news –

POPPY. What? What?

TESSA. Suzie's father passed away.

POPPY. Ohhh / – when?

TESSA. When was it Thursday. Thursday.

POPPY. Ohhh.

TESSA. Yeah. Had a heart attack. So we're gonna get a card an' just send it.

POPPY. Humm –

Beat.

TESSA. Yeah. You don't know what to say though. You know what I mean. All you can do is offer yer sympathy an' yer support an' that's about that really. (*Beat*.) So that was that.

Pause. POPPY *changes into her negligee*. TESSA *notices scratches and burns on* POPPY*'s arm*.

Oh yeah, what did – you – do that?

POPPY. Uumm –

Beat. POPPY *bursts into laughter.*

TESSA. Come on –

POPPY (*laughing*). Deliberately, all right? Jus' say / deliberately.

TESSA. Oh, all right then –

POPPY. Mm.

TESSA. – o-kaaay. (*Beat. Laughing.*) What are you / *like*?

POPPY. Burns.

Beat.

TESSA. We're gonna stop smoking, next.

POPPY. Yeah, I know.

TESSA. Then duh-take all sharp implelements away. / (*Laughs.*)

POPPY. Nah, fine – I've 'ad me funny five minutes. (*Beat.*) Just feeling *crap* (*Beat.*) – ya know (*Beat.*) – nothing in particular, everything all at once, probably.

TESSA (*a little slurred*). Yeah we've all 'ave our vices / – uhhh –

POPPY. Mm. I'm two weeks – two months behind on my rent.

Pause.

TESSA. Come on, dick'ead (*Beat.*) – let's get you over an' done with.

Pause.

The doorbell rings.

Beat.

(*Whispering*). Oh, good. (*Beat.*) Yeah. That's – Dickbrain.

POPPY. Oh. (*Beat.*) / You want me to get 'im in, or –

TESSA. Yeah, go on – le' 'im in (*Beat.*) – yeah. (*Beat.*)

POPPY *goes to open the door and let him in. The punter,* DICKBRAIN, *enters.*

DICKBRAIN. Gosh (*Beat*.) – Are you new?

Pause.

POPPY. No, I've been 'ere a while – but (*Beat*.) – / erm –

DICKBRAIN. Sorry, you are?

POPPY. I'm, Poppy.

DICKBRAIN. Oh, Poppy, right – so I've met, uh (*Beat*.) – I'm due
– to see, um –

POPPY. Tessa – yeah –

DICKBRAIN. Tessa, yep.

POPPY. Come this way.

DICKBRAIN. Shall I come, with you (*Beat*.) – did you say come
with you?

POPPY. Yep.

DICKBRAIN. Oh, right – okay –

POPPY *leaves him in the hallway. She re-enters the sitting
room, and* TESSA *exits to the hallway.*

TESSA. He-*llooo*.

DICKBRAIN. Gosh, this is the real, Tessa – isn't it?

TESSA. Uhh, yeah – disappointing, though.

DICKBRAIN. What?

TESSA. Ohh-I'm gonna have to say (*Beat*.) – no –

DICKBRAIN. What, now?

TESSA. Yeah, I know you've booked –

DICKBRAIN. Tessa. Second time.

TESSA. No-no-no-no, it's just that, I don't, think –

DICKBRAIN. No.

TESSA. – I can do – any more, what you want – me to do.

DICKBRAIN. Really?

TESSA. Mm.

DICKBRAIN. Can you say why? (*Beat*.) Disappointing, / that –

TESSA. Uuuhhh –

DICKBRAIN. You've got some / restriction –

TESSA. Yeah (*Beat*.) – it's just / I don't, wanna –

DICKBRAIN. Or, you don't like, what I do.

TESSA. Uh, it's not that, it's just I (*Beat*.) – no, I'd rather not.

DICKBRAIN. Oh – a shame.

TESSA. Sorry –

DICKBRAIN. Can't you say any more than that?

TESSA. No I've thought a lot about it, that's why I said come round. I thought –

DICKBRAIN. What is it particularly (*Beat*.) – / this (*Re: her breast*.) or – I know –

TESSA. Y-y-eah (*Beat*.) – yeah, I (*Beat*.) – yeah –

DICKBRAIN. We used to enjoy / – a fair bit of fun, there –

TESSA. Yeah, I can't be as forthcoming, shall / we say –

DICKBRAIN. Ahhh – right. (*Softly*.) Ah dear.

TESSA. Sorry. But I thought I'd do – rather do it face to face.

DICKBRAIN. No well. I acknowledge what you're doing. You couldn't just do one and call it a day.

TESSA. N-no sorry.

DICKBRAIN. Ah come on. You do it for me, you know what I'm tryin' to say.

TESSA. N-n-no-no.

DICKBRAIN. You 'ave –

TESSA. I have, / I 'ave changed, an awful lot –

DICKBRAIN. – you 'ave – you've become a hard lady, haven't you?

TESSA. I have become a very hard lady –

DICKBRAIN. Oh come on. For old time's –

TESSA. Eum-mm –

DICKBRAIN. That leaves me a bit zilch for this afternoon doesn't it, / yeah –

TESSA. Sorry.

DICKBRAIN. What about the other young lady?

TESSA. No she wouldn't no.

DICKBRAIN (*hopeful*). Wouldn't?

TESSA. No. No – she's very shy.

DICKBRAIN. Oh, / dear, and I've made so – s-*such* an effort – too –

TESSA. Sorry.

DICKBRAIN. – no. (*Beat.*) It – would've been nice if we could've just 'ad / a farewell –

TESSA. Mm. (*Beat.*) No, / I've thought about, thought about – no-no-no –

DICKBRAIN. – ca – can – ja-, just, just – *just* a farewell.

TESSA. Nope.

DICKBRAIN. One for the road.

TESSA. Nope.

DICKBRAIN. Gosh, you *have* changed.

TESSA. Yes, an awful lot, mm.

TESSA *starts to laugh.*

DICKBRAIN. Oh, yeah, I c'n – I *don't*, know quite, what to say, 'ere –

TESSA *is laughing louder now.*

– an' I'm all, keyed up to go –

TESSA. Sorry.

DICKBRAIN (*quietly*). Where do I go?

TESSA. I haven't got a clue.

DICKBRAIN. No that's no-[t] / very helpful is it either?

TESSA. That's the only thing I don't know.

DICKBRAIN. Mmm. I don't know what to say there.

TESSA (*brightly*). Okey cokey. Then I wouldn't wanna waste yer money and yer time –

She starts to lead him out.

DICKBRAIN. And there, was I, looking forward to seeing you, / and –

TESSA. Sorry. (*Laughs.*)

DICKBRAIN. There we were, not doing it.

TESSA. Sorry about that, but / thank you very much – take care. (*A kiss.*) M-wah.

DICKBRAIN. Very well, goodbye. Yeah, and you, look after yourself.

TESSA. I / will do, bye-bye!

DICKBRAIN. Okay, cheers (*Beat.*) – right.

TESSA shuts the door behind him.

TESSA. Mm.

She comes back in.

Hee-hee-hee. Fuck off. He said 'My God you have changed.' I said 'Yes I have.' (*Beat.*) For the better I believe.

POPPY. Mmm.

Beat.

TESSA. Fuck you, you arsehole. (*Beat.*) You're not worth it.

Scene Six – The Girlfriend Experience

Lunchtime. 10th October 2007. SUZIE *has just come out of a booking.* POPPY *is sitting in the chair stage left, downing pints of cider and pints of water. She drinks very heavily throughout the scene until her client arrives.*

SUZIE (*to* TESSA). Look at you all smiling, look –

> TESSA *giggles.*

> So did 'e stay over?

TESSA. No – no – he just came up here / – this morning.

SUZIE. Just popped in. (*Beat.*) An' it's all – going well.

TESSA. It's – seven weeks today, / yeah –

SUZIE. Ooh my God, and counting.

TESSA. And counting. (*Beat.*) S'our anniversary.

SUZIE. I just go an' have a quick freshen up, is that all right?

TESSA. Yeah, yeah. (*Beat.*) Yeah, anything to put it off. / (*Giggles.*)

SUZIE (*under her breath*). 'Anything to' – she says –

> *They giggle.*

> SUZIE *exits to the bathroom.*

TESSA. Uh-I got meself a boyfriend. (*Beat.*) Mm. His name's Corey. (*Beat.*) He knows what I do. (*Beat.*) 'E's gorgeous, 'e's about – (*Blows out a breath. Pause.*) 'e's just gorgeous, uuumm – (*Laughs loudly. Laughing.*) 'e's – ll-lovely. (*Beat.*) I met 'im at, Hard Johnny's, which is the pool hall. (*Laughs.*) An' he's so *ll-lovely* (*Beat.*) – so *lovely*! (*Beat.*) An' we walked *back*, 'e walked me back 'ome (*Beat.*) – al-long the seafront we held hands! (*Giggles.*) Ooh-ooh-hoo-hoo! (*Laughing.*) I 'aven't held hands in *years*! (*Chuckles.*) Oh, it was gorgeous. It's like a being putty – in one's hands. (*Chuckles.*)

POPPY. Can I 'ave some more water, then? I gotta wee at two o'clock. (*Laughs.*) So you have to get full-up, y'know. (*Pause.*) Do you think tha's enough?

She holds up a three-litre bottle of Frosty Jack's cider. TESSA
*chuckles and goes to the kitchen to get her another pint of
water.*

(*Clears her throat.*) Three litres (*Beat.*) – f-hive, point two eight
p-pints. (*Sighs.*) An' it's not even *cold*. Yeah. And then 'e won't
turn up, d'ya know wha' I mean?

POPPY *continues to drink heavily.*

SUZIE *re-enters.*

TESSA. So how's your lovelife, anyway?

SUZIE. Oh that's off – I, finished it. (*Beat.*) Just – well very
simple, really – there's a few things I wasn't happy about.
(*Beat.*) I hadn't seen 'im for a li'le while, an' all he could think
about was just going straight to *bed*, an' I didn't want that – I
needed his support (*Beat.*) – I needed a hug – and a cuddle.
(*Beat.*) An' I think he kinda fell in love with Suzie – he – didn't
fall in love with the real me. (*Beat.*) Cuz 'e expected me to be
up to sex the whole time (*Beat. Sniffs.*) – and, you know. (*Beat.*)
But, yeah, he we had a bit of an upset – (*Under her breath.*)
bastard. (*Beat.*) I, cuz I found, on my computer – he'd done,
he'd done a video – phone, from 'is phone of himself – (*Lowers
her voice.*) *wanking.* (*Beat.*) Right – an', it was on my c-cuz
'e'd *down*loaded it onto the computer, an' I'd cuz he – writes
poetry, an' 'e put it in 'is poetry folder, on my computer. (*Beat.*)
Thought, 'Ooh let me just', cuz he'd men-[tioned] he did a
poem about Dad, you see, so I jus' g-, I was cleaning and
dusting, he was worki-[ng] at work – 'n' I thought I'll just read,
this, an' it was la-[st], n-not this Wednesday gone, Wednesday
before – just read the, y'ow the poem, that 'e did fer Dad, and,
um (*Beat.*) – I opened up the folder, an' was these two *videos* on
– I – goes 'Oh', I thought 'Wha's 'e downloading bloody porn
again – on my', I've told 'im not to, on my computer in case it
gets a *virus*. (*Beat.*) So, opened it up, aaand – there's him
(*Lowers her voice.*) *wanking.* (*Beat.*) He's looking jus' down his
body, *wanking* – think 'Okay, yeah, fine.' An' at the end, it says
'I hope you like what you see, Shirley.' (*Beat.*) But h-it's in my
living room, cuz you can see my sofa, an' see my carpet – and
so it was done were *while*, we were *together*.

TESSA *sighs.*

So he came through the door, last Wednesday – okay – an' I said
to 'im, 'Derek, d'you love me?' (*Beat.*) 'Yeah, yeah' he says –
'why, what 'ave you done?' (*Beat. Laughs.*) I said 'Well s'not
what *I've* done – s'what you've (*Lowers her voice.*) *fucking
done*,' I said. (*Beat.*) He said 'What, what what?' (*Beat.*) And, I
so, 'e said, and 'e kindof then tried to deny it – that it didn't
exist, and I said I *showed* it to 'im, and then it was like the
words – like – 'I hope you like what you see, Shirley' cuz 'e's
got a friend called Shirley 'oo lives in Crawley. (*Beat.*) 'E says
to me – 'Well I did it to cheer 'er up' – 'e's 'cuz her
granddaughter's gone into hospital.' (*Beat.*) I said 'T'cheer a
friend up you send them chocolates a joke or some flowers
(*Beat.*) – or so-[mething]' I said 'you *don't*, send 'em a, *fucking
wanking* video, in *my living room*.' (*Beat.*) Y'know. (*Beat.*) So I
kicked 'im out. (*Beat.*) I don't *need* that.

TESSA. No. (*Beat.*) No.

SUZIE. An' I think he kinda fell in love with Suzie – he didn't fall
in love with Stacey – the real me. (*Beat.*) Cuz he expected me to
be up for sex the whole time. We've all got home lives. We've
got stresses an' pressures and bills to pay –

TESSA. Yeah / – no –

SUZIE. These guys, you know, they don't, they don't *want* our
problems, and what's going on –

TESSA. No, they just / (*Beat.*) – want the nice part.

SUZIE. They *want* (*Beat.*) – us to be happy. (*Beat.*) SUZIE. Come
on then, Tess.

She claps her hands together.

TESSA. Oh – God – (*Sighs. Beat.*) Lot's developed, said the L-
word / – there we go –

SUZIE. Ooh – both of you?

TESSA. Yep, mm –

SUZIE. Oh my *God*! (*Beat.*)

TESSA. Oh! (*Beat.*) We have, a *song*.

Pause.

Seven weeks 'n' we got a song! (*Gapes*.)

They laugh.

SUZIE. Well Derek an' I had programmes.

TESSA. Oh did ya / (*Beat*.) – ohhh!

SUZIE *laughs*.

All / right then – okay –

SUZIE. We like *Mur-*, we like *Murphy's Law*.

POPPY *burps*.

POPPY. Oh. Pardon me.

TESSA. Oh yeah – I can't cum.

SUZIE. You / can't cum?

TESSA. I can't cum with other *clients* –

SUZIE. What, since bein' wi' Corey?

TESSA. Yeah. (*Beat*.) Even wiv Plunger Man, yesterday. (*Beat*.)
And his tongue is *legendary*.

Pause.

He's always in the back of my *mind*. (*Beat*.) I've got ta stop
thinkin' about him. (*Beat*.) If he said (*Beat*.) – 'I want you to
give it up.' (*Pause*.) I'd seriously think about it.

SUZIE. You gonna get changed, then?

TESSA. Yy-*yeeeesss*!

SUZIE *laughs*.

SUZIE. It's ten / to two!

TESSA (*laughs*). I know! Has it made any difference (*Beat*.) – /
nooo!

SUZIE. *Nooo!*

TESSA. I'm in love, I'm not allowed to do people –

POPPY. I wanna go soon.

TESSA, I should think so.

POPPY. Well I'll give it to ten past two then I'm gonna have to go, but I'm like getting there now – don't say the 'wee' word. (*Burps*.)

TESSA. Uum – yeah-yeah oh – more exciting *stuff*.

She goes over to the mantlepiece and picks up a piece of paper. Pause.

My daughter's results.

SUZIE. Oh, I saw the *cards* – so I was thinkin' I was gonna ask / you.

TESSA *lets out a half-hysterical, half-excited, high-pitched giggle.*

TESSA. Hee-hee-hoo-hoo-*hoooo*! (*Beat*.) Sorry. (*Clears her throat*.) Hm.

SUZIE. Oh my *God*!

TESSA. I / know!

SUZIE. Oh, my / *Go-oood*!

TESSA. I know!

TESSA *is clapping her hands, laughing excitedly.*

SUZIE. That's bloody fan/tastic –

TESSA. Isn't it fantastic. (*Beat*.) See! –

SUZIE. English Lit –

TESSA (*breathy, mock-seductive voice*). So hookers *can* do it, you see? We can have –

SUZIE. In German, my *Go-ood* / (*Beat*.) – she got German –

TESSA. – a (*Beat*.) – a good *family* life, an' bring up children-in-the *right way*.

POPPY. Oh no. I can't hold it.

TESSA. You're gonna have to start again.

POPPY. Yeah. Dammit!

She rushes out to relieve herself in the bathroom.

SUZIE. I was sayin' I saw this really lovely guy who was new to seein' an escort. I saw him on Thursday for an hour. An' he – I spoke to him an' he said 'Oh I bin tryin' to get hold of you in ages.' I said 'Oh my dad died da-da-der.' He ss-[aid] – he said 'Oh you sure you want to work?' I said 'Well yeah – ' I said 'cuz I need to work – I need to be busy.' He bought this really lovely kind – of – a-a – a contact number for a counsellor an' also a little book on bereavement an' stuff. An' it was jus' li-[ke] – it was jus' so nice. An' he was so *tender* an' compassionate. I mean it wasn't the full thing. Ya know he didn't come an' do the full thing. But it, but is was jus' – an' he said – that was fine, it was as much as he wanted. An' it was just absolutely lovely. (*Beat.*) Feel a bit lost at the moment, I'm not really, sure / (*Beat.*) – where I'm – meant to be, I'm kinda like – mmm. Yeah a bit kind of lost-ish.

TESSA. No – no, yeah – yeah – bit, bit *numb* (*Beat.*) – round the edges – yeah –

POPPY *re-enters.*

POPPY. There's no way I'm gonna be ready in five ten minutes.

TESSA. No.

SUZIE. I just bin. I can't go.

POPPY *downs another pint.*

POPPY. Urgh – God –

TESSA *laughs.*

– I can' 'ave much more a that, I 'an't even *eaten*, much, so I'm gonna be absolutely / (*Beat.*) Yeah, I might need summore water.

TESSA. Pissed.

TESSA *goes into the kitchen and re-enters with a pint of water.*

POPPY. One?

TESSA. Nah, I got two. I can only carry one, fucking hell.

POPPY (*under her breath*). Ooh. I've just done a really stinky one. (*Chuckles. Laughing.*) Sorry, eh (*Beat.*) – my tummy's upset

now, as well, guh – ooh, God, it's like the dog (*Beat.*) – sorry.
(*Belches.*) Pardon *me* – sorry. (*Beat.*) Bubbles (*Beat.*) – they get
there eventually. (*Laughing.*) Ha-ha-ha-ha-better that way, than
the other –

POPPY *laughs.* SUZIE *sprays her Charlie body spray in*
POPPY*'s direction.*

Hoh.

The doorbell rings. POPPY *gets up to answer it.*

I'm still not there yet – it's / like *flippin' 'eck!*

TESSA. Oh.

POPPY *greets* TERRY, *the punter, in the hallway.*

POPPY. How are you.

TERRY. All right, thank you.

POPPY. You been 'ere before?

TERRY. No.

POPPY. Nope?

TERRY. Nope.

POPPY. Are you lookin' for anyone in particular, or are you the
one / (*Beat.*) – did you phone before?

TERRY. No. Uuhhh (*Beat.*) – I did. (*Beat.*) Uumm. (*Beat.*) Poppy –

Beat.

POPPY. Poppy watersports. (*Beat.*) *Yes*, that's me.

TERRY. That's you is it?

POPPY. *That's* me.

Beat.

TERRY. We'll see how it goes.

TERRY *claps his hands together in anticipation.*

POPPY. Okay.

POPPY *takes him into the bathroom.*

Pause.

SUZIE. Let's hear yer love song then.

TESSA turns on her CD player.

TESSA. Play – why is it not playing?

'What About Now' by Chris Daughtry, starts to play.

SUZIE. And so he's dedicated this song to you –

TESSA. Okay y'gotta-listen-to-the-words now.

SUZIE makes a turkey 'gobble' sound.

It's the *next* bit that's like – quite –

The song continues to play.

Yep.

She beats her hand on her heart.

SUZIE. Made my toes curl, that / did.

TESSA. Like – (*Gasps.*)

Song plays.

Int it *lovely*?

SUZIE. This is how 'e *feels*.

TESSA. The only thing I can think of is if he walked away now,
I'd be fucking absolutely devastated. It would hurt me, a lot,
and I know that, and I think that's what sort of going woah.
(*Laughs.*) Barriers. (*Laughs.*)

*POPPY comes out of the bedroom with TERRY as the song is
still playing.*

TERRY. Look like I bin dragged though a hed-[ge] backwards.
(*Laughs gently.*)

POPPY. Well there's a mirror in there anyway. (*Laughing.*) So you
can check that. (*Laughs heartily.*)

TERRY. Anyway thank you very much. / Yeah. See you later on.

POPPY. All right. Thank you. Bye.

TERRY. Bye-bye.

POPPY sees him out sighs, and goes back into the sitting room.

POPPY. I did it, I *did it*! Yaaaaay! Poppy did it! (*Beat*.) She shoots, she *scoooores*!

They laugh.

Ah, I'm so (*Beat*.) – so *proud* (*Laughing*.) I managed ta do it! / (*Chuckles*.)

SUZIE. I'm not bloody surprised after all that, you 'ad (*Laughing*.) to *drink*.

Pause as they wait for the song to end.

TESSA. He's always in the back of my mind. (*Beat*.) I've got ta stop thinkin' about him. (*Beat*.) If he said (*Beat*.) – 'I want you to give it up' I'd seriously think about it. I said it (*Beat*.) – I-I, I'm *not* – me, when I do it. (*Beat*.) I-it's (*Beat*.) – actress Tessa, it's (*Beat*.) – i-it makes me (*Beat*.) – be able to disappear (*Beat*.) – I said, 'Because I don't, like (*Beat*.) – the *real me*.' (*Beat*.) An' 'e was like, 'You don't 'ave ta hide, any more.' (*Pause*.) Ohh, fuckin' 'ell. (*Beat. Gasps*.) He said 'You're real – in here (*Indicates heart*.) – and you're in *here*,' (*Indicates inside the room*.) – He said 'I just didn't *know*, you were out *there*.' (*Indicates outside the flat. Beat. Laughing, excited*.) 'Ow roman*tic* is *that*?! (*Draws breath. Lets it out*.) Hooo! (*Laughs heartily for a few beats*.) Put *that* on your fuckin' *stage*!

They all start to laugh, TESSA *especially*.

What d'ya say to that, *what* / do ya *say* to that?

The phone rings.

TESSA. Go 'way.

TESSA *chuckles, then goes to answer it. She immediately takes on her businesslike telephone voice*.

He-*llo* can I *help* you? (*Beat*.) Yes, certainly – uh, we're based – uuhh, just off of Bournemouth seafront, any good? (*Beat*.) I got three *lovely* ladies today, uh, we've got-uh, Suzie (*Beat*.) – she's, uh-thirty-*seven*, auburn-haired – big blue eyes – very much the 'Girlfriend Experience'. (*Beat*.) She's lovely an' busty an' curvy – she's a forty double-D, size eighteen stature. (*Beat*.) Oh yeah, quite a handful (*Beat*.) – uuhh, then we have Poppy – she's a lovely redhead – she's a, pretty thirty-two-year-old, she's quite tall, she's five-nine five-*ten* (*Beat*.) – also busty and curvy, a forty double-D, size eigh*teen*. (*Beat*.) Then we've got Tessa, she's a very striking brunette she's thirty-eight, years of age – she's very busty, she's a forty double-F – nice curvy fourteen stature, an' about five-*seven*, tall. (*Pause*.) Yep – or breast relief, whichever you wish. (*Beat. Speaking deliberately*.) Or *breast relief*. (*Pause. Brightly*.) Seven o'clock this evening. (*Pause*.) Yep. (*Beat*.) *O*-kay, *cool*. (*Beat*.) Thank you, bye!

They return to watching the television.

The End.